MORE THAN WORDS

MORE THAN WORDS

Prayer and Ritual
for Inclusive Communities

Janet Schaffran, CDP
and
Pat Kozak, CSJ

MEYER
STONE
BOOKS

First edition © 1986 by Pat Kozak, CSJ, and Janet Schaffran, CDP; second revised edition © 1988 by Pat Kozak, CSJ, and Janet Schaffran, CDP. All rights reserved.

Published in the United States by Meyer-Stone Books, a division of Meyer, Stone, and Company, Inc., 714 South Humphrey, Oak Park, IL 60304

Cover design: Carol Evans-Smith

Manufactured in the United States of America
92 91 90 89 88   5 4 3 2 1

Library of Congress Cataloging in Publication Data

Schaffran, Janet, 1945-
    More than words.

    Bibliography: p.
    1. Prayers.   2. Liturgies.   3. Symbolism.
4. Ritual.   5. Language question in the church.
I. Kozak, Pat, 1947-   II. Title.
BV245.S314   1988   264'.13   87-62871
ISBN 0-940989-30-1 (pbk.)
ISBN 0-940989-33-6 (spiral)

Contents

Preface

I<small>T IS OUR HOPE</small> that the prayers and rituals of this book will be of practical help to individuals and communities. Consequently, we give permission for the reprinting of any part of this book not expressly written by others. When using our material, we do ask that you credit the source, i.e., *More Than Words,* by Janet Schaffran, CDP, and Pat Kozak, CSJ, published by Meyer-Stone Books. This permission does not include use for profit or inclusion of this material in other collections.

To reprint material that is copyrighted by others, it is necessary to contact the authors themselves. We encourage you to do so.

We encourage the creative adaptation of these prayers to the needs, time constraints, and diverse backgrounds of those who gather to pray.

We have tried to identify sources used in the book, and, when possible, we have secured permission for their use. We apologize if we have inadvertently overlooked or misidentified authorship; in any future publication of this material, we will be happy to correct any such oversight.

We are grateful for the permissions we received to reprint and share the gifts of others.

Finally, we give thanks for all those whose lives and faith and friendship have helped to shape this book and who continue to shape our lives.

P<small>AT AND</small> J<small>ANET</small>

Acknowledgments

The authors gratefully acknowledge permission to quote from other sources as follows:

"Rest in My Wings," by Colleen Fulmer, from *Cry of Ramah* (cassette and music book), available from Loretto Spirituality Network, 529 Pomona Avenue, Albany, CA 94706 (p. 55).

The Clowns of God, by Morris West, copyright © 1981 William Morrow & Co., Inc. (pp. 57–58).

Guerrillas of Grace, by Ted Loder, copyright © 1984 by LuraMedia, San Diego, Calif. (pp. 63–64, 106).

"For Those in a Wintry Season," copyright © 1985 by Sally Dyck (pp. 67–68).

"Litany of Naming," by Diann Neu. Water Publications (pp. 70–71).

"Sister," words and music by Cris Williamson, copyright © 1975 Olivia Records, Inc. (BMF), Bird Ankles Music, Inc. (p. 73).

Seasons of Your Heart, by Macrina Wiederkehr, OSB, copyright © 1979 Silver Burdett Company (pp. 75–76).

The Indian Council in the Valley of the Walla Walla, 1855, by Lawrence Kip, p. 22 (pp. 81–82).

"A New Eucharistic Prayer," by John Page, in *America*, February 16, 1985. Reprinted with permission of America Press, Inc., 106 West 56th St., New York, NY 10019. Copyright © 1985 (pp. 83–84).

"They Have Threatened Us with Resurrection," in Julia Esquivel, *Threatened with Resurrection*, copyright © 1982 by Brethren Press (pp. 85–87)

"[Echoes]," by Diann L. Neu, in *Women Church Celebrations*, published by Water (pp. 85–87).

"Psalm 146" (pp. 87–88) and reading on pp. 100–102, by Bob Hoover, in *Central American Reflections*, Religious Task Force on Central America, Wesley Foundation, United Methodist Church.

"In the Company of the Faithful," by Vincent Harding, from *Sojourners*, May 22, 1985. Reprinted with permission from Sojourners, Box 29272, Washington, DC 20017 (pp. 89–92, 123–127).

"Faith and Imagination: The Holy Spirit and the Ministry of the Church," copyright © 1979 by Sally Dyck (pp. 93–95).

"Death Notice" (p. 99) and the reading on pp. 117–118, from *Not Just Yes and Amen: Christians with a Cause*, by Dorothee Soelle and Fulbert Steffensky, copyright © 1985 by Fortress Press.

"The Four Elements" (p. 104) and the mediation on pp. 104–105, from *Views from the Intersection: Poems and Mediations*, by Virginia Ramey Mollenkott and Catherine Barry. New York: Crossroad Publishers, 1984.

"A Psalm Reflection," from *Psalms from Prison*, by Benjamin F. Chavis, Jr. Reprinted by permission of Pilgrim Press, copyright © 1983 by Benjamin F. Chavis, Jr. (pp. 108–109)

"River Water for Sale," from *Song of the Bird*, by Anthony de Mello, SJ, copyright © 1982 by Anthony de Mello, SJ. Reprinted by permission of Doubleday & Co., Inc. (p. 114).

"El Shaddai," by Colleen Fulmer (pp. 129–130).

Reading used by permission of Rita Petruziello, CSJ (p. 130).

Lyrics from "Mantle of Light," by Colleen Fulmer (p. 133).

Reading adapted from William W. Warren, *History of the Ojibway People*, reprint ed., St. Paul: Minnesota Historical Society Press, 1984 (pp. 142–143).

"Blessed Is She," copyright © by Colleen Fulmer (pp. 140–141).

From *A Gentle Presence*, copyright © 1977 by Chuck Lathrop (pp. 142–143, 148–150, 159–162).

Reading from Ohiyesa, adapted from *The Soul of the Indian*, 1911, by Charles A. Eastman, reprinted by permission of the University of Nebraska Press. Copyright © 1911 by Charles Alexander Eastman (pp. 144–145).

Introduction

WHY ANOTHER BOOK? Why the present concern about the style of our worship? Why the interest in the manner of our prayer together? And why are people increasingly involved in discussions about inclusive language, simplicity of life, justice, cultural pluralism, images of God?

The answer might well be found in the experience of canoeing. In canoeing a river, it is possible to go in either of two directions, with the current or against it. Obviously, paddling downstream with the current is the fastest and easiest method. It is also possible to rest in the canoe, with little or no paddling, and allow the current to carry the canoe downstream.

A second direction and method is to paddle against the current, and so travel upstream. This approach, however, requires considerable and consistent effort. Even a short pause in the paddling will result in the canoe being turned around and propelled downstream by the current.

It becomes clear that while it is possible to travel almost effortlessly, passively downstream with the current, it is impossible to travel passively upstream against the current. Such canoeing is merely wishful thinking.

If we apply this analogy to change in our church and society, a similar truth is evident. The prevailing "current" in our society and church encompasses racism, sexism, and ageism, to name but a few of the injustices that plague us. While our participation in these evils may sometimes be unconscious and unintended, it is nonetheless real, and is the cause of continued suffering and injustice.

It is not the intention of this book to address the causes of these evils nor argue their existence. Nor is this the place to consider to what degree these are conscious or unconscious realities in our lives. We regard the existence and power of these evils as a given and believe they constitute the prevailing climate, a current, if you will, in church and society. And just as in canoeing, choices are available.

We can choose to paddle with the current, adding by our own efforts and intention to the racism, sexism, and other injustices already present. A second choice we have is simply to travel with the current, passively allowing ourselves to be carried along by it, and become, even if unconsciously and unintentionally, part of its movement and direction, which is to say, part of its injustice and oppression. Or we can actively work against it, with energy and commitment, striving to travel upstream against the current, hoping eventually to arrive in some better place.

In working for change, as in canoeing, it is best to have someone with us to help with the paddling. It is difficult to maintain consistent effort alone. This book, particularly its prayer services and rituals, is intended for communities — for gatherings of folks intent on paddling upstream together.

Part I

Concepts and Values

Inclusive Language

WORDS ARE ONE OF THE PRIMARY WAYS by which we connect with each other. We come to communicate via words; we come to understanding, even to solidarity, through the not-so-simple ways in which sounds are arranged in sequence. Much of this is arbitrary. How did one word come to mean one thing and not another? Why is one word appropriate and another not? To what degree are words and their meanings a matter of social convention?

Inclusive language is not a fad. It is not this year's "cause," to be soon replaced by another. The growing use of inclusive language is the result of a serious commitment on the part of many people to use words more responsibly, to speak more precisely, and to communicate more truthfully and sensitively.

Many books have been written concerning the development of language from a variety of perspectives. For the interested reader, they are well worth the time and effort to read and integrate. It is our intention, however, simply to address the questions, "Why do we bother with inclusive language?" and "How much is involved in this 'inclusivity'?"

We are affected both consciously and unconsciously by the language we hear and use. It would seem that repeated use of words develops a certain immunity, a resistance to their meaning and impact. Such words, then, have minimal effect: crass words no longer jar us, slang becomes acceptable, scientific and military terms are adapted to daily experiences without notice. However, there is much to suggest that this is not the case. We are not unaffected by words, and our seeming freedom and ease with particular usage is perhaps more the result of numbness and verbal satiation than matured sensitivity.

Language is always influential and formative, but it may be especially influential in times of prayer, because at these times, ideally, the whole person is involved — through speech and hearing, through sight and touch and movement. People are often more relaxed, receptive, less on guard and hence more susceptible to the variety of messages being conveyed. More of the experience is likely to be absorbed, both consciously and unconsciously. This receptivity may facilitate an experience of community support, a recognition of the holiness of God, or a realization of the beauty of our own humanness. However, such positive experiences are not always the result.

Imagine a concelebrated liturgy in a church where the vast majority of worshippers are black. Imagine this liturgy concelebrated by five white male priests, gathered around the altar, wearing colorful vestments and proclaiming, "We are a holy race, a royal priesthood..." (Preface to the Fourth Eucharistic Prayer, Roman Liturgy). What does a black child see and experience at such a liturgy? White men proclaiming that they are a holy race? Are blacks unholy? Unworthy? What does a young black girl see and experience? She sees only men, only white men, dressed in special robes. Can only white men belong to this holy race, to this royalty and priesthood? Are all blacks and all women unholy and unworthy?

In this experience, the reason for the concelebration does not matter. The origin of the particular translation of the Eucharistic prayer or its tradition does not matter. The richness of the original Scripture from which the passage was drawn does not matter. These reasons and insights are all unknown to the child. In this situation, the question remains: What does the black child or adult experience at this liturgy? The question is significant because liturgy is not intended to be first and foremost a cognitive experience. It is, instead, an experience and expression of faith.

What do we expect a child to understand when we teach that "God loved men so much that He himself was born a man in order to come to earth and be with us"? Are we unconsciously teaching that it is better to be a man than a woman? If God, who is wise, chose to become a man, did God choose the better of two options?

We are increasingly aware of the impact that verbal abuse, insulting name-calling, and minimizing humor can have on a person in the development of self-concept or in the perception of that person's environment.

Non-inclusive language does similar damage. An unwillingness on the part of church people to use inclusive language is especially difficult to understand because of all the times and places to use words responsibly and sensitively, common prayer and public worship would seem to merit a priority of care and attention.

What about the charge that inclusive language is simply an over-reaction? Doesn't everyone already understand what is meant by the words used so that any change in language is really unnecessary?

> What about "We hold these truths to be self-evident, that all men are created equal...with certain inalienable rights"? If our "fore-fathers" who wrote these words understood "men" to be inclusive of women, why did it require a constitutional amendment for women to vote? If "men" is understood to mean all people, why did it take years of struggle, congressional legislation, and police protection for black sisters and brothers to be able to vote? The truth is that "men" has not always been an inclusive term and continues even today to be restrictive in meaning. In the interests of clarity and charity, the use of inclusive language is necessary.

What about the charge of "tradition"? After all, we have always said it this way. People have grown accustomed to it and have some feeling about it.

> This charge holds a strange mixture of fact and fiction, of merit and nonsense. Simple convention does not constitute a tradition, and having done something before should never be the primary reason for doing it again. The question needs to be asked: What truth or value does this action or passage express? It would seem more respectful of persons to assume their desire to communicate honestly and clearly rather than assume their inability or unwillingness to change and to grow.

What about the charge "but the author wrote it this way and a change in the text will destroy the poetry and flow of the passage"?

> It is important to safeguard the quality of a translation and to preserve the delicacy of style of a particular text. And it *is* possible to do this. It is possible to modify the wording in a way that maintains the harmony and grace of a passage and at the same

time avoids jarring the reader or listener with an uneven or unnatural paraphrase. Any author must necessarily write from within a particular culture. His or her writing may well represent the best of that culture. Adapting the language of a given passage may very possibly be more consistent with the author's efforts to communicate sensitively than an insistence on retaining exclusive and inaccurate expressions. It is hard to imagine that the great writers, preachers, composers, and believers of earlier times, among them, Jesus, Sojourner Truth, Anne Hutchinson, and John XXIII, would object.

What about the charge that changing the language is inconvenient?

It is true. It is time-consuming and it is inconvenient. And so too is living the gospel. Something is sadly missing when inconvenience becomes the criterion for our actions.

Any word, any language, is a human invention. It has not come down directly from "on high," but rather out of the "stuff" of our human situation, human history, and human cultures. Our hearts, our lives, our words, and our world are all on the way, all in the process of redemption and transformation. The only constant word is the Word made flesh, and that is the one Word that crosses cultures and time. That Word, that person, still calls us to conversion and to change.

In the following section, as well as in the prayer services themselves, we offer examples of common changes toward inclusive language for use in prayer.

Symbols and Rituals

RITUAL IS AN INTEGRAL PART OF LIFE, common to all creatures. It provides the actions and forms through which people meet, carry out social activities, celebrate, and commemorate. Whether actions performed appear casual or dramatic, sacred or secular, they express a meaning and significance that extend beyond the particular event itself.

Rituals express the truths by which we live, the relationships and beliefs that underlie our lives. Rituals, like the way we greet each other, the blessing before sharing a meal, the expression of thanks when receiving a gift, the spoken or kissed "good night" at the end of the day, all carry a significance greater than mere social conformity.

As a faith community we have a need for rituals that convey the power and significance of the present moment and situate that moment within the context of our shared faith. One such example is the long held ritual we celebrate on the occasion of a birthday. I still recall the third birthday of a nephew. The family, parents, siblings, aunts, and uncles were gathered around the table while the three-year-old celebrant stood perched on a chair, face aglow with the candlelight. He looked excitedly from face to face while we sang to him. When he was finally told, "Make a wish!" the child, with sheer delight, blew out the candles to the sound of enthusiastic applause. The mystery of life was once more celebrated. Given gratuitously, age is not merited or earned in any way. Life and time are gifts of a gracious God, witnessed to and celebrated by those who are bonded in love.

It may be necessary to adapt the action or the ritual to allow for fuller and more meaningful participation. It may be helpful to change the setting, the physical arrangements, in order to accommodate the number of people and to enable their meaningful and comfortable presence. It might be advantageous to prepare the place of the gathering to make the atmosphere more conducive and supportive of the ritual prayer.

We are sensual people and the more our senses are involved, the more likely we are to be fully involved as whole persons. So color, lighting, acoustics, movement, seating, and logistics all merit some attention. Their particular use and adaptation will be influenced by the words and style of the prayer, by the occasion of the gathering, by the number of people present, and by the practical limitations of space, time, and resources. Part II will offer specific examples and suggest ways in which these concerns might be expressed.

One last comment regarding the variety of elements involved in any ritual. There is a need today to reaffirm the human, to celebrate the natural wisdom and beauty to be found within creation. It is a way of giving witness to our faith that "because of creation, and still more the Incarnation, nothing is profane." The human person is made in the image of God and continues to reveal divinity in and through the sometimes subtle, always profound mystery of humanity. The created universe, since its first birthing, was charged with the breath and Spirit of God. "It was good" from its very origin. The "stuff" of our physical lives, our bodies and our world, is sacred. The more we can incorporate and express this belief in our common prayer, the greater the capacity this prayer possesses to root us in the goodness and mystery of our God.

The use of gesture and movement, of dance and mime, restores a connectedness with our own bodies. The use of earth symbols such as water and air, earth and fire, re-establishes our rootedness in this awesome and fragile planet on which we make our home.

We are in need of a greater ability, perhaps even a greater willingness, to live symbolically. However, this calls for some caution because living symbolically does not mean that we surround ourselves with objects and signs or claim that the ultimate revelation has been given in each and every event of our lives. An appreciation of symbols requires a reflective presence, a realization that there is always more present than what meets the eye. It requires that we recognize that God has become involved with us and in our world, and that our human experience, in the context of such faith, has lasting significance.

If rituals are to be meaningful, persons must first believe that their experiences are true and worthy of reflection. These reflected-upon experiences are then shared with the community as stories of faith and finally celebrated as experiences of faith, grace, and power. Such celebrations become festivals of incarnation, redemption, and our ongoing resurrection; they mark our own passage to greater and fuller life.

It is important that rituals and symbols not be contrived. If a lot of words are needed to explain a symbol, do not use it. Either the symbol lacks the power and clarity to speak for itself or the experience of the community is limited and they are unable to make the connection that links ritual with life.

Go slowly at first. Use what is most common and natural, what is already experientially part of people's lives: water, light, fire, darkness, earth, bread, and wine. Build on these to enable people to slow down the inner pace of their lives and to recognize a rhythm and truth there. This enables an appreciation of the symbolic as well as the ability to express oneself and one's faith in ritual. This eventual expression of faith is a strengthening of the individual and of the community.

We are long overdue for a change, for movement from the too-often-sterile places and styles of prayer, devoid of any sign of a good and gracious God. We are long overdue for a change, for movement from the too-often-inhospitable places and styles of prayer, where "community" and "family" are far from the experience of the believers who gather. We are long overdue for a change, for movement from the too frequent uniformity of our worship to a profound sensitivity that acknowledges the exquisite beauty and mystery of our humanness, the richness or our diversity, and our capacity to manifest the power and glory of God.

There is good reason to believe that this long overdue change can begin now; in fact, it has already begun.

Images of God

WHO IS OUR GOD? It is a timeless question, always in search of a personalized response.

Who is God *for me?*

How do I describe my own experience of God?

In what or whom do I believe?

What is my image of God?

As believers, we possess communal stories of faith, the religious myths of Judaism, Christianity, and Islam, an awesome variety of religious traditions that offer a wealth of images of God. Within these dominant images of God, Christ, and Allah, for example, are countless other images: the Divine as Creator, Warrior, Liberator, Redeemer, Shepherd and Spirit, to name a few.

It is not by chance that particular images are prevalent in our traditions. They have been selected from among a limitless variety, all expressing a human (and sometimes inspired) interpretation of a human experience of God. But there are sociological and cultural realities, as well as religious, that influence the emergence of a dominant image of God. At the time of the Exodus, God was hailed as a liberator. In times of destitute poverty, God is the one who prepares a banquet. In a patriarchal culture, the dominant images will be male. In an oppressive society, the oppressors will often preach a God who urges obedience and rewards long-suffering, while the oppressed will look to a God who saves and liberates.

This is not to suggest that any of these images is wrong or necessarily negative, although their exclusive use might be. Each of these images conveys something of the truth of our experience of God. Each image is the result of a unique blending of our communal and personal experiences set in a particular time in history in which we are both descendants and ancestors, inheritors and benefactors.

Any image of God, however, is incomplete. Even our use of the word "God" might seem to limit its referents to male images, thereby eliminating powerful images of the Divine as feminine. It is critical that we no longer restrict God to any one dominant image or expression. The human person has need of a deeper awareness and fuller experience of God. And in the service of truth, God deserves a more inclusive portrayal, for God is far greater than any or all of our images.

What determines the truth and the appropriateness of a particular image of God? What makes an image "fit"? The image used must be consistent with what we believe about God, a belief that is enlightened by contemporary studies in Scripture and theology. But in addition to what might seem like academic criteria for determining the appropriateness of images, other questions are helpful. What images of God are life-giving for us personally and for our world? Which images encourage growth? Which images challenge us to respond with compassion and justice? What images enable us to view God and the world from the perspective of the poor and oppressed? Which images nurture and sustain intimacy?

The wealth of possible images of God is limited only by our own imagination and our own hesitation to reflect on our experience and draw the connections between concrete human situations and faith.

These images can be evoked in a variety of ways: through dance and storytelling, mime, journaling, nature, music and art. Images are invoked or sustained in virtually every human experience. They range from images of the majesty and power of God that might be suggested by a thunderstorm to the image of a welcoming friend or vindictive judge anticipated at the hour of death.

An image of God held at the age of five that remains largely unchanged at the age of forty reveals very little about a God of infinite love and response. It does, however, reveal something tragic about that individual's lack of growth and inability to experience and reflect upon God's action in his or her own life.

Active imagination and personal reflectivity are involved in the development of new images of God. Working with clay might well be an experience of holding ourselves, with utmost care and attention, in our own hands — as God holds us. Or it might be an experience of being refashioned over and over again as we are healed and made whole by a God who loves us.

A ballet, with its strain of effort, dramatic expression, and grace, might nurture an image begun in Romans 8, where all creation is seen standing on tiptoe, straining for that fulfillment to be found in God.

Time given to an experience of nature might put us in touch with the fountain of life deep within us or help us to claim the mystery and beauty of our own darkness.

The birth of a baby may connect us to the scriptural images of God as a midwife or to the life-giving capacity within us. It might renew our call and responsibility to work for a peace based on justice that would insure a future for all the children of the earth.

These images are sometimes specifically concerned with our God images. Other times the images evoked are expressive of our images of ourselves or of the world as we perceive it. The concrete expression we give to faith and the choices we make concerning lifestyle are functions of the interplay of our image of God, our self-image, and our world image. Consequently, the development of positive, life-giving images is vital for adult faith.

This use of the imagination involves openness to being influenced by something or someone outside of ourselves in order to learn life's meaning, depth, and possibilities. We will be creating new images of God. In the process, we are changed. We grow. We respond to a God who is revealed in a marvelous variety of ways. Through these new images of God we find ourselves challenged to live, to love, and to act justly.

Cultural Pluralism

WHAT DOES IT MEAN for us as people of the United States to pray as members of the church? What does it mean to pray as members of the world community? As a global family? We often use these terms glibly, though sincerely, assuming our own awareness of the beauty and diversity of these communities. We assume a cognitive and affective acceptance of the peoples of these communities.

But is this assumption true? Are we aware of the culturally distinct peoples within our local communities? Are we attentive to the significant numbers of Hispanic, African, Asian, and Native American persons who make their home in the United States? Are we aware that the U.S. population represents only 6 percent of the population of the earth?

And what does this reality have to do with how we pray?

Our prayer is expressive of who we are and what we believe, what we have experienced and what we hope for. It is important that this "who we are" be understood as broadly as possible. We are a global family and as such share in the wisdom and experience of the entire community of believers. Without this realization, we pray as less than ourselves, lacking an awareness of the power and rootedness and solidarity that could be ours.

What does it mean to pray with an awareness and appreciation of the cultural pluralism that exists within this body of believers? To begin with, it might mean that we pray differently when we pray as a community. When we gather for common prayer or formal worship, we often rely on materials that are highly verbal and minimize feeling and color or the possibility of spontaneous expression. We generally draw on the writings of white persons and make use of white music and white voices, whether spoken or sung. Our prayer services typically manifest a Western system of logic characterized by its linear progression and rational tone.

All this is strikingly inconsistent with any avowed appreciation for cultural diversity and pluralism. The occasional inclusion of writings of a South American theologian or Native American poetry or black music, however well intentioned, is sadly inadequate. Sporadic use of these sources only serves to perpetuate a situation of inequality and unconscious prejudice.

If we are to be taken seriously as members of a global family and universal Body of Christ, it is essential that our prayer reflect this identity, at least in our efforts to be multicultural.

How much is necessary? To what limits of pluralism and inclusion are we called? In Psalm 137, we pray, "Though there our captors asked of us lyrics of our songs, and our despoilers urged us to be joyous: 'Sing for us the songs of Zion!' How could we sing a song to our God in a foreign land?" This is true of us today as it was for the Israelites more than two thousand years ago. In order to share our prayer we need to feel at home, comfortable, at least minimally at ease with the people and situations around us.

It is important to expand the range of our familiarity beyond the mainstream of our own culture to its margins and marginated people. We need to become familiar with other cultures even within our U.S. American culture.

For example, we might use excerpts from the writings of Martin Luther King, Jr., at times other than Black Culture Week. It is too easy to relegate the wisdom and power of this Christian to one setting or one issue. Why not draw on his writings on faith or perseverance or non-violence or public witness? These values are not restricted to the black community alone; they are his gift to a world community.

What about using the music of Central America and providing the translation and pronunciation? The songs of these present-day ministers of the Word proclaim a belief in the resurrection, a vibrant hope in the face of persecution, and a profound regard for the poor.

Why not use the art and poetry of Africans, of Native Americans, and of Appalachians?

Why not make ample use of the silence of the Quakers and Asian peoples?

Why not make use of the feminine style and image, voice and leadership?

Our liturgy in words and in ritual has become impoverished by our own reliance on the so-called majority culture. Our dependence on one culture has diminished us. We have lost touch with the richness and wisdom of our sisters and brothers throughout the earth.

We have come to rely on and expect certain words, symbols, and rituals used in liturgy. Yet if Eucharist is our daily bread, are not tortillas a clearer, truer sign of daily nourishment in Central America than the traditional eucharistic bread? If we are celebrating the gathering of a community for worship, doesn't the dance of many cultures convey the gathering of people far better than a staid procession? What distinguishes tradition that is imposed on a people from tradition that is expressive of a people and its culture? To whom belongs the right and responsibility to answer such questions?

It is no small thing to begin to try to pray as members of a global family. It would be a hope worthy of our calling and identity if one day sisters and brothers of cultures quite distinct from each other would join together in prayer. All would know they are family. Then as in Psalm 137, we could sing a song to our God. It would be no foreign land in which we are gathered. It would be home.

Language Regarding "Darkness and Light"

One general comment regarding imagery and cultural pluralism is in order. It is important to use imagery of darkness and light with extreme care. Light and dark are commonly used as synonyms for day and night, for white and black. They are usually mutually exclusive and often used to symbolize good and evil. When used this way, such imagery is an example of real, though unintended racism.

Guided reflections that ask us to recall our experience of darkness and sin may unconsciously perpetuate racist stereotyping of white as good and black as bad. It is true that darkness may symbolize chaos, isolation, loss, and fear. It also symbolizes mystery, depth, intimacy, and waiting. Light, while often implying positive qualities, can also suggest barrenness, cold isolation, and lack of warmth. Rather than rely always on the images of dark and light to convey a desired meaning, it may be a better practice to use another word that more accurately and sensitively communicates the meaning intended in the prayer.

This is not to say that darkness may never be used responsibly to represent the negative or painful experiences of life; only that the image should not be used exclusively that way. The image of light may be used to convey life, truth, and goodness; the truth of our own human experience validates the use of the imagery of light to communicate experiences of pain, exposure, and stark abandonment as well.

An example of the need for sensitivity is found in the first letter of John: "God is light; in God there is no darkness." How is this passage heard, given our familiarity with the "dark continent," the "dark races," and dark-skinned peoples? Obviously the author is not intending or promoting racism. If the intention of the passage is to contrast truth and deceit or to contrast hatred and love, it is appropriate for us to make use of words that might more effectively convey the original meaning. Imagery is to be at the service of truth. Because of this, the actual words used are always subordinate to the truth being revealed.

Part II

Examples

Inclusive Language

As ANYONE WHO HAS STRUGGLED to change non-inclusive language knows, it is often more difficult to adapt language than it first appears. The choice of revision will first depend upon the context. For example, the number of syllables and the accent are important to note if the change to be made is in a song. A casual gathering of believers will allow some revisions that would be inappropriate in a formal assembly, while the literary style of the passage, particularly poetry, will dictate some words rather than others.

Changes in language can be divided into four types:

1. Adding a female reference to an exclusively male reference, e.g., adding "and sisters" to "brothers," or changing "he" or "his" to "he/she" and "his/her."

2. Deleting of the exclusive word, e.g., changing "we have known his mercy" to "we have known mercy."

3. Substituting an appropriate synonym, e.g., "mankind" becomes "humankind," "kinsmen" becomes "kinspeople," "family," or "relatives."

4. Finding an alternate way of expressing the same concept, e.g., "Merciful Father" can be changed to "Compassionate God," "God of mercy," "Source of all mercy"; or the line "And crown thy good with brotherhood" might be changed to "And make of us one family."

The following are examples of changes that can be made to incorporate inclusive language into common prayer. While not all-encompassing, they offer suggestions for options in language change.

If the text reads:	Change to:
God...he made the heavens	God...you made the heavens God...who made the heavens
God...his love is everlasting	God...whose love is everlasting God...your love is everlasting God...this love is everlasting
We have known his mercy	We have known God's mercy We have known your mercy We have known this mercy We have known mercy
From the power of sinful men	Power of sinful men and women power of sin power of the sinful power of sinful ones
This man...his	Man and woman...their they...their people...their all...their
Spokesman	Spokesperson representative
Clergyman	Clergyperson minister cleric
God become man	God became human The one who was divine became human
Brotherhood	Family unity

Son

Son and daughter
child/children
first-born (if appropriate)

Watchman

Guard
sentry
sentinel

Kingdom of God

Reign of God
God's dream for all creation

A further guide on the topic of inclusive language is *Cleaning Up Sexist Language,* a booklet published by the Eighth Day Center in Chicago. It offers a thorough rationale for and extensive practical examples of inclusive language.

Symbols and Rituals

LISTED BELOW are common themes in prayer. For each theme possible symbols and rituals are indicated.

Focus of Prayer   **Symbols and Rituals**

Birth and Naming   *Symbols:*

Egg, balloons, earth (soil or clay), personally naming another, a mirror to image self, a tree, pictures of contemporary prophetic people.

Rituals:

Telling what your name means or the ritual expression of a clown.

Hope   *Symbols:*

Clover (three- or four-leaf), sheafs of wheat, wildflowers, globe (hope for global awareness), seeds, evergreen branches, shells, a wreath entwined with weeds and flowers, a bird, Japanese cranes.

Rituals:

Mime, body movement expressing reaching out, circular movements.

Justice-Seeking People	*Symbols:*
	A globe or large map, clippings of recent newspaper articles, a bag of clothes.

Rituals:

Four readers for the service — one from the North, South, East, and West, sharing a variety of breads and crackers representing diversity of peoples and cultures.

Death — Life *Symbols:*

Fall leaves, pictures of death/life, wall-hanging or tapestry from various countries (e.g., El Salvador, Brazil, Northern Ireland), a wreath, a stain of blood, water, branches, a red piece of cloth, wind and light, pictures or symbols "in memory of" experiences or people.

Rituals:

Use of fire to consume or transform, moving from one prayer space to another — symbolizing "new life."

New Life *Symbols:*

Brightly colored eggs, flowing water, flowers, colored sashes from various cultures, food, Bible.

Rituals:

Lighting fire, circle dance rituals, gesture prayer outside facing the sun, ritual sharing of what gives life, what is life-giving today for you.

Service

Symbols:

Wine, bread, foods that are festive, hospitality, God's Word, maypole, garden tools, wood carving tools, crafts, painted faces, cord or twine symbolizing weaving together lives of service, ceramic pots, homemade shawl.

Rituals:

Praying a blessing over each other, washing of hands, cooking a simple meal and inviting another and eating together.

Images of God

THESE LISTS, meant to help evoke new and fresh images of God, are not seen as complete or final. As you read the titles or phrases, allow your personal images of God to surface. Some titles are original, while many are drawn from books included in the bibliography.

Title or Image	Focus or Theme of Service
Gentle One	Creation, forgiveness
Justice Seeker	Peace, world issues, powerlessness
Builder God	Future concerns, purpose for the Christian
Seeker of Silence	Thanksgiving, reflections of life's inner movements and blessings
Giver of Hope	In loss or separation, in loneliness, in new beginnings, in struggles
Compassionate One	Forgiveness in times of pain, in failure, in weakness
Parent of the Poor	For concerns of oppression, for refugees, for sanctuary

God of Miracles

In experiencing generosity of an individual, group, or country, when in awe, in moving out of confusion into clarity

Additional Titles or Images of God

Nurturing Names	Earth Images
Gentle One	Timeless God
Forgiving One	God of Wonder
Giver of Gifts	God of Dawn
Precious One	Gentle One of the Earth
Healer	Breath of Life
Gracious	Breath Within
Holy One Who Gathers Us	Evening Warmth
Loving One of Wondrous Stories	Evening Breeze
Mother of My Heart	Giver of Life
Tenderness	Mother and Father of this Earth
Comforter	Creator
Companion	Earth Maker
Warm Center	Holy Light
Presence	God of all Seasons
Bakerwoman God	Womb of All
Birthing God	Breath of the Cosmos

Majestic Names	Personal Images
Eternal One	Lover
God of Power	Mother
God of History	Father
Graced One	Eternal Friend
Eternal God	Silent One
Spirit Within	Tender One
Provident God	Gentle Friend
Gracious Spirit	Amazing Grace
Lord of Wondrous Patience	Persistent Friend
Best Counselor	Enabling Friend
God of Wonder	God of Our Struggle
Wonder Worker	Jesus Healer
Word of God	Jesus our Brother
Gift of Life	Keeper of Promises
Mystery	Loyal One
Glorious One	Befriender of the Friendless

General Names	Liberating Names
God of Dreams	Just One
God of Children	Liberating Friend
Mystery of Love	God of Inner Peace
God of all Trust	Liberator

God of all Hope

Insistent One

Dreamer of Dreams

Holy One Who Breaks Bread

Giver of Hope

O God of Endings

Lord of Laughter

Lord of Tears

Ingenious God

Seeker of Silence

God of Miracles

Amazing One

Endlessly Eager One

Present One

Questioning One

God of Struggle

Compassionate God

Justice Seeker

Liberating and Loving Friend

Challenger God

Risk Taker

God of Justice

Seeker of Justice and Joy

Doer of Justice

Suffering God

Daring One

Peace for the Frightened

Freedom of the Oppressed

Parent of the Poor

God of the Defeated

Cultural Pluralism

THERE FOLLOWS a list of themes frequently chosen for community prayer. Opposite each theme is a resource drawn from a culture other than the dominant white American. These resources, songs, readings, and rituals can be incorporated into the prayer experience. If this listing is "successful," it will have sparked still greater creativity in the reader, who will find these resources to be only a beginning.

Theme	Resource
God's faithful love	Relate to the faithful love of the mothers of the disappeared of Central and South America; Colleen Fulmer's song "Mothers of the Plaza de Mayo"; relate to concern for missing children in the United States
The power of visioning, dreaming to bring about New Creation (or God's Reign of Justice, peace)	Excerpts from "I Have a Dream" speech of Martin Luther King Jr., August 28, 1963
The role of discipline to clarify our focus	Explanation of the ritual of the "sweat lodge" in Native American cultures

The human family	Inviting those present to pray the Lord's Prayer together, encouraging people to pray it aloud in whatever language they know
Solidarity with the oppressed	The song "Singing for Our Lives" by Holly Near, adding appropriate verses
Observance of Hiroshima Day (anniversary of bombing)	Instrumental music by Japanese composer Kitaro
Strength of the human spirit against all odds	Vietnamese poetry set to music in the song "The Rock Will Wear Away," by Cris Williamson
Stewardship or sanctuary	Native American readings on the sacredness of the earth, the land as a gift to be shared; use excerpts of "This Land Is Home to Me," a pastoral letter on powerlessness in Appalachia by the Catholic bishops of the region
The gospel as counter-cultural	Daily headlines
Perseverance/hope	Story of Rosa Park's refusal to give up her seat on Montgomery bus and subsequent city-wide bus boycott; its part in the Civil Rights movement
God as Nurturer, Bakerwoman	Breads, foods of many lands and cultures
Fullness and mystery of life	Steady drum beat (in many African cultures, the drum expresses the heartbeat of all living things, humans, animals, and the earth mother)

Part III

Guidelines for Preparing a Prayer Service

Guidelines
for Preparing a Prayer Service

For PREPARATION OF A PRAYER SERVICE, the following four questions are suggested as an overall guide.

1. What are we celebrating?

2. Who will be there?

3. How can we help those present to experience the celebration that is taking place?

4. In what way will people participate in the event or ritual?

What follows is an attempt to "walk through" the preparation of one prayer service. Imagine that it is being created by a few folks upon the celebration of the death of a close friend. The four questions stated above will be used as a guide.

1. What are we celebrating or commemorating?

   The death of a friend.

2. Who will be there?

   Close family and friends. Possibly a support group that meets weekly.

3. How can we help people experience and understand what we are celebrating or commemorating?

Storytelling about the times spent with the deceased friend. Use prayers, poems, readings, and songs that were important to the friend.

4. In what ways will people participate in the event or ritual?

Through the sharing of stories. Through listening, singing, and gestures. It is important that everyone, including children, be able to participate.

After considering the answers to the four questions above, it will be helpful to reflect on the elements from Part I in preparing this service for a friend.

Inclusive Language
Symbols and Rituals
Images of God
Cultural Pluralism

- How can we be aware of inclusive language?

Read over the prayers and songs to make certain that the language used is inclusive.

- What symbols can be used?

Use symbols and rituals that relate to the experiences of this friend or to the loss of this person at this time.

Use a candle, a living plant or flower, a photo of the friend, sharing a favorite food of the person, expressions of warmth and affection.

- What images of God come forth?

God of tears; Womb of mystery; Compassionate One; Cause of our joy.

- How can we be aware of cultural pluralism?

Recall how people of other cultures celebrate death. How might their rituals be expressed with regard to the one who has died?

If the person enjoyed gardening, celebrate a return to Mother Earth. Use a reading or ritual from our Native American sisters and brothers. If the friend was Irish, use an Irish Blessing.

- How can we physically arrange the prayer area?

Select a gathering-place that is conducive to personal sharing and allows for a comfortable setting for children as well as adults.

A living room or a large room with chairs and pillows arranged in a defined space should be appropriate. Let the space you gather in be expressive of the prayer.

We have described a process that can be used in preparing a service for almost any occasion. The guide is meant to help integrate concepts that are useful in calling forth others to prayer. Use this guide as you prepare to gather people of various cultures, those who experience diversity in experiences and lifestyles as well as those whose conceptions of and relationships with God vary. It is our hope that +through these gatherings, all of us will come to know and love the depth and length and breadth that is God.

Part IV

Prayers

Invitations to Prayer

Leader: In the name of our God who shares divinity with us,
in the name of our God who shares humanity with us,
in the name of our God who unsettles and inspires us,
let us give praise and thanks!

All: Amen!

•

Leader: We give thanks, God of wonder,
for the marvel of creation that surrounds us,

All: And for all the wonders of life we have known.

Leader: Let us see your glory, your justice, and your peace.

All: May our lives and our world be reawakened
by the power of your grace.

•

Leader: Come to our aid, Compassionate One.

All: We have need of your mercy.

Leader: Listen to us now as we pray.

All: Open our eyes to your works,
and our ears to your words of life.

Leader: In the presence of a God whose word
has called the stars into being,

All: We stand in awe.

Leader: In the presence of a God whose arms have held children,
whose eyes have sparkled with laughter,

All: We stand in trust.

Leader: In the presence of a God whose breath
has stirred within us and caused our hearts
to thirst for love,

All: We stand in need.

Leader: Before you, Giver of Life, we come in faith,
in search of love and truth and wholeness.

All: Be with us; hear us, we pray.

•

Leader: We give you thanks, God our Creator,

All: Because you have given us life.

Leader: You have made us in your image
and breathed your Spirit into us.

All: We are alive with divinity
and your glory is made manifest in us;
we have been touched by God!

•

Leader: Show us your mercy, God of our struggle,

All: We are in need of your strength.

Leader: Show us your face,
you who have given us birth.

All: Look upon us; restore us to wholeness.
In your name, we pray.

Gathering and Concluding Prayers

God, our creator and sustainer,
you loved us long before we knew ourselves to be lovable
and love us still.
Give us, we pray,
a greater awareness of your love for all people,
and a confidence in the action of your grace
in us and in your church.
Inspire us with a greater sensitivity
to the poor and oppressed.
Give us the courage to act on their behalf.
We praise you today
for your mysterious ways among us:
for your presence in the midst of human affairs
and your seeming absence.
By the power of your Spirit,
may we grow in the truth that impels us to act justly,
and thus give expression to the compassion of your child, Jesus.
This we ask through this same Jesus Christ,
who lives among us as friend and savior.
Amen.

•

We give you thanks,
God of abundant life,
for bread and friendship and hope.
With these gifts of your grace we are nourished.

With these signs of your presence we are able to be faithful.
Continue then to nourish us, inspire us, and call us,
that we might help make your Reign
more of a reality in our day.
Amen.

•

Hear us, we pray, God of our longing.
We have searched for you
and seen only our own shadow on the ground.
We have called to you
and heard only silence.

Come quickly
or else the emptiness of our longing
will turn us inward on ourselves.
Keep our blinded eyes turned toward you
that we might recognize your presence
when your glory breaks through at last.
On that day we will know again
what we have known so often and yet so rarely:
You have been in our midst all along.

•

Good and gracious God,
who are we that you have loved us so well?
When we find our own selves so often difficult to trust,
how is it that you have given us this world of yours,
each other, and a future that is in our hands?

We have need of your compassion, your power, and your wisdom.
Our own has once again proven inadequate
in the face of so much need.

Be strong in us. Purify our intentions.
Deepen our commitment.
Be for us all that we need. Be God for us.
We await your saving presence.

•

We pray to you, our good and gracious God,
as a people who cherish the memories that are ours,
and who claim a common history as a sacred gift.

We ask you to renew your grace in us,
that we might recognize your presence in our midst
and hear the call of the gospel
in the human needs that surround us.

Through the power of your compelling Spirit
may we grow in courage,
that our actions might reflect
the love we profess.
We ask this in the name of your child, Jesus.
Amen.

•

How long, God of justice, how long
before you hear the cries of your people?
How long will the poor be hungry
before they are fed?
How long will children fear death
before you hold them in your arms?
How long must the weak suffer
at the hands of their oppressors?

What keeps you from acting?
For your name's sake we ask!
Father of the Poor. Mother of Mercy.
God of all consolation!
Your silence makes mockery of your name.
Come, God of Justice.
Too much suffering, too many deaths.
You have waited long enough!
Strike quickly in our world
and today
in our hearts.

•

Loving Creator,
we ask for wholeness for ourselves and for your church.
Do not allow fear, ignorance or pride
to limit the action of your Spirit,
nor allow mere custom to prevent
the divine creativity within us
from bearing fruit.
We ask for the insight to understand
the needs of people today,
that we might grasp the complexity
of the situations that face us
and the absolute simplicity of human need:
the poor have a right to hear the gospel,
the hungry a right to food,
the oppressed a right to freedom.

Enable all of us to be women and men
enthusiastic for your ministry,
contagious in our love
and eager to be among your people as ones who serve.
This we ask through Jesus Christ,
who came as brother and servant to us all.
Amen.

●

God of our hope,
we give thanks for this day and these people,
and for your gospel that gives this day meaning
and provides your people direction.
Stay close to us.
Do not pass from our view
lest we lose our way, and our heart.
Encourage us, root us in you.
Make us desire your life in us
that our only fear is your absence,
and our greatest joy is your love.

●

God of faithfulness,
we come to you at the end of a day,
and find ourselves needing to begin again
on new projects and new ideas.
We are in need of energy and renewed hope.

What change are we able to effect
by all our words or actions or prayer?
What do our efforts matter?
We are in need of your grace
to unsettle and redirect our hearts.
We are in need of your power
to rekindle and sustain our passion for justice.
We are in need of your love
that we might recognize the ever-present possibility
for change and conversion and growth.

We believe your Spirit is at work in our world.
Give us eyes of faith
that we might see such wonders in our midst
and the courage to live in hope.

Prayers of Reconciliation

Leader: Aware of our weakness and confident of your mercy,
we pray:
For seeking simply to replace
the one who presides at our community tables
rather than working to restore
the dignity of the community, we ask:

All: Show us your mercy.

Leader: For our unwillingness to trust the powerful spirit of God
within each other, we ask:

All: Show us your mercy

Leader: For our fearful hesitation to follow Christ
wherever the integrity of the gospel might lead us,
we pray:

All: Show us your mercy.

All: Compassionate God, we seek to be a church
and find ourselves in need of your help.
Be gentle with us, please;
you know the sincerity of our efforts,
our fears and our repeated failures.

Be strong with us as well;
you know our weakness and our pride,
our attachment to prestige and position.

Make us women and men of the gospel,
that the hopes and dreams you have for your world
might be more fully realized in our day.
Amen.

•

All: Loving God, you are just and compassionate;
be with us today.
We look to the future, to the days ahead of us,
and yet we know we have need already
of forgiveness and healing.

- We ask forgiveness of you, our God,
  and the forgiveness of those gathered here,
  for becoming impatient when we were too busy,
  too distracted, too much in a hurry.

- We ask forgiveness
  for being too quick to speak or act,
  for not taking time to think or to pray.

- We ask forgiveness
  for falling into the same mistakes again and again,
  which cause hurt to others and to ourselves.

- We ask forgiveness
  for taking too much time,
  for wasting time before we act,
  for being concerned
  about appearances and approval,
  for not trusting in your own absolute love for us.

- We ask forgiveness
  for the smallness of mind in our thoughts,
  for a narrowness of heart in our actions.
  Help us to accept others
  who think and act differently from us.

- We ask forgiveness
  for letting fatigue discourage us,
  for becoming cynical

about the worth of our own efforts
and the power of your grace,
for minimizing the urgency of the gospel.

Leader: Loving God,
you know our weakness
and the extent of our failure
to love you and one another.
You see the sincerity of our efforts as well.
Look upon us who have been offended
and lift up our hearts.
Look upon us who have given offense
and help us heal the hurt we have caused.
As we willingly,
with your help,
forgive one another.
We ask you to forgive us
and fill us with your healing power and grace.

All: Amen.

Psalm Prayers

Lift up your hearts.
God has loved you with a tenderness beyond words.
Our God has remembered your faithfulness
and put aside your sin.

Lift up your hearts.
God has called you, believing in your goodness.
God has given you a new season of hope
and cast aside despair.

Lift up your hearts.
for God's Word will not return empty or void.
It will accomplish the task for which it was set.

Lift up your hearts.
for God's Word is alive within us,
and we are unable to be silent.
We will sing the truth with our every breath.

We lift up our hearts to our God;
for we have known full well God's justice and mercy.
What return can we make for all God's goodness?
We will lift up our hearts
And reach out our hands to the poor.

—Inspired by Psalm 50

•

One thing I ask of God; this I seek:
to dwell in the house of our God
all the days of my life.
That I may see beauty in every leaf and rock
and feel the breath of God in the evening breeze.

I want to look on the face of God
and see truth as it really is;
to know God with my mind's eye
and love God with all my heart.
So will I ponder God's Word day and night,
and wait with it, until it comes to life in me.

One thing I ask of our God; this I seek:
to walk in the way of truth
all the days of my life,
to follow this most powerful of spirits
wherever she may lead.

With strength and compassion
I will give myself in service,
And hold everything in an open hand.

One thing I ask of God; this I seek:
to dwell in the house of our God
all the days of my life.

One thing I ask of God; this I seek:
to walk in truth
all the days of my life.

> One thing I ask of our God, this I seek:
> God alone,
> all the days of my life.

—Inspired by Psalm 27

Bread-Breaking Prayers

We have shared bread and wine many times in our lives,
in many places, for many reasons.

The bread that we now break and the cup that we take
are a sharing in the life of Christ.

May our acceptance of it today be a sign of our faith

- in the ongoing goodness of a God who journeys with us,

- in the power of love to remove any barrier
  within and among us,

- in the mystery of the call given to each one here,
  to make bread and life and beauty available to everyone.

We pray then, good and gracious God,
that we might recognize you in this breaking of bread today.

It is the bread of heaven,
  the bread of the poor,
  the bread of our lives.
May we recognize you
  every time we join someone on a journey,
  every time we share a meal,
  every time we take bread into our hands.

And may this recognition call forth such a joy in us
that we might never lose sight of your goodness.

May it inspire such love in us that our hearts
might continue to burn within us,
keeping alive your memory and your promise.

And may it provoke such a longing for truth in us
that we will never be satisfied
until the whole earth experiences
your justice and your peace.

Let us share this bread and wine as Jesus taught us,
knowing that our lives are forever changed
by this and every breaking of bread.

— Written for the 25th Jubilee Celebration
of Marietta Fahey, SHF

•

As bread that was scattered on the hillside,
was gathered together and made one,
so too, we, your people,
scattered throughout the world,
are gathered together around your table
and become one.

As grapes grown in the field
are gathered together and pressed into wine,
so too are we drawn together
and pressed by our times to share a common lot
and are transformed into your life-blood
for all.

So let us prepare to eat and drink
as Jesus taught us:
inviting the stranger to our table
and welcoming the poor.
May their absence serve to remind us
of the divisions this Eucharist seeks to heal.
And may their presence help transform us
into the Body of Christ we share.

— Adapted from the Didache

Part V

Prayer Services

Needs and Expectations

Leader: Come to me, you who are tired,
you who are burdened, come.

All: We come with our hopes and our fears;
we come as we are.

Leader: I have loved you with an everlasting love.
From your mother's womb,
I have taken delight in you.

All: We come in joy and in need;
we come as we are.

Leader: Today is the acceptable time,
now is the hour of salvation.
All who are burdened, come.

All: Today is the acceptable time,
Now is the hour of salvation.
We come as we are.

SONG

"Rest in My Wings," by Colleen Fulmer, or other appropriate song.

Refrain:

Don't be afraid, I'm holding you close in the darkness.
My love and my grace will carry you through the long night;
The life that I give bubbles in you like a fountain,
So rest in my wings and put all your fears to flight.

Tho you be burdened, I will cradle you deep in my nest.
Tho you be weary, my wings will enfold you in rest.
Tho you be desert, my rivers will flow deep inside.
Tho you be barren, I'll fill out your womb with new life.

Tho you be orphaned, I'll always be here at your side.
Tho you be empty, I'll bring forth new fruit on the vine.
Tho you be thirsty, you'll drink from the well of my side.
Tho you be hungry, the finest of bread I'll provide.

— From "Rest in My Wings,"
by Colleen Fulmer

REFLECTION

Gentle One who walked this earth,
Why is it that our needs embarrass us so?
Why do we try so hard to be self-sufficient,
as if being by ourselves, untouched,
unnurtured by another is our goal?

We seem threatened by our need.
Our interdependence frightens us.
And we pretend, with the emperor,
that we are richly clad.

The tailors knew the truth
though they kept silent.
The children knew
and as children will, they shout the truth
lest rocks themselves call forth.

If truth be told, then all are free!
The locks are sprung.
the doors flung open.

All that waits is that we stand and walk
(like "Stand and walk. Be healed!" of years gone by)
and find that sharing common sun and sky
is fine dependence.
Unlike the emperor, we're chilled without
the royal disguise and find
we must take shelter
with each other where
much to our surprise
our needs and we are held.

— Pat Kozak, CSJ

BRIEF QUIET

READING: *Jeremiah 29:11–14a*

OPPORTUNITY FOR SHARING AND PRAYER

CLOSING PRAYER

All: We give you thanks,
Gentle One who has touched our soul.
You have loved us from the moment of our first waking
and have held us in joy and in grief.
Stay with us, we pray.
Grace us with your presence
and with it, the fullness of our own humanity.
Help us claim our strength and need,
our awesomeness and fragile beauty,
that encouraged by the truth
we might work to restore
compassion to the human family
and renew the face of the earth.
Amen.

Blessing Cup in a Nuclear Age

PREPARATION

A bottle of wine and goblet are needed.

INTRODUCTION

Leader: In the novel *The Clowns of God,* Morris West introduces us to Jean Marie, the recently elected pope who has been given a vision of the end of the world as we know it, an end tragically brought about by nuclear holocaust. He has written an encyclical to all people of faith in the hope of changing the direction in which nations and all humankind are moving, thus averting the final catastrophe that Jean-Marie has already seen.

    In this excerpt from the encyclical, Jean-Marie describes the aftermath of the war.

Reader: ... It is clear that in the days of universal calamity the traditional structure of society will not survive. There will be a ferocious struggle for the simplest needs of life — food, water, fuel, and shelter. Authority will be usurped by the strong and the cruel. Large urban societies will fragment themselves into tribal groups, each hostile to the other. Rural areas will be subject to pillage. The human person will be as much a prey as the beasts whom we now slaughter for food. Reason will be so clouded that [people] will resort for solace to the crudest and most violent forms of magic. It will be hard, even for those founded most strongly in the Promise of the Lord, to sustain their faith and continue to give witness, as they must do, even to the end.... How then must Christians comport themselves in these days of trial and terror?

... Since they will no longer be able to maintain themselves as large groups, they must divide themselves into small communities, each capable of sustaining itself by the exercise of a common faith and a true mutual charity. Their Christian witness must be given by spreading that charity outwards to those who are not of the faith, by aiding the distressed, by sharing even their most meager means with those who are most deprived. When the priestly hierarchy can no longer function, they will elect to themselves ministers and teachers who will maintain the Word in its integrity, and continue to conduct the Eucharist....

— From *The Clowns of God,*
by Morris West, p. 35

Leader: Let's imagine, for just a short time, that what was written in *The Clowns of God* has happened.

Let's imagine, for just a short time, that the bombs have been dropped, that the world as we know it has been destroyed.

Take a moment to try to comprehend what that might mean. What would have taken place around us? What would it mean for us to be the sole survivors of a nuclear war?

All of our families would be gone — all dead. Our homes, all the places with which we are familiar — all destroyed.

We have only each other left. Perhaps we know each other from before; perhaps we would have just come upon each other in the months after the destruction. Perhaps, too, some of those whom we first met have since died, victims of the insanity we call nuclear warfare.

So we come together with each other: wanting yesterday never to have happened; wishing we could wake up tomorrow and find this to have been only a nightmare. And yet, we are here.

We made a decision to gather today, because after all these weeks and months, we find ourselves in need of trying to gather together the faith that we share, to find support in what each other believes.

We find ourselves wanting to celebrate the Eucharist, like so many times of old, like so many times in the past. And yet, we look around and see that we have no priests; we have no books, no sacred vessels. We have no bread. It has long since been contaminated or destroyed.

But still we have each other. We have the memory that is ours. We have this common cup that we have found. We have some wine — and the memory that is ours of someone who did this before, ages and ages ago, who gathered together some friends of his, survivors of a sort, and sought to gain from them, share with them, some hope, some support, some strength that would enable them to face the night ahead.

And so, perhaps today, we could do just that, in his memory, and by so remembering, make him present once again.

We have no books, no Scriptures. We must rely on each other for the words of faith that will help us. We need each other to remember. We have only what we share together.

What do we remember of what Jesus said so long ago? What do we remember from Scripture? What words of faith? . . . of hope? What words of life? I need you to remember for me, because all I remember is that he told us we are to love our enemies, and I don't know if I can do that now.

Leader invites those present to share what they remember of the words of Jesus — e.g., "I remember when he told us . . . " No discussion, simply the sharing of the Word. Be comfortable with the quiet that settles over the group.

BLESSING PRAYER

Leader: We ask you, Good God, to bless this wine, to bless this cup that we offer to you and to bless us even as you bless this cup.

We need to feel your closeness, your presence with us. We need to feel more deeply the bonds that draw us and tie us to each other. We remember that once upon a time, many years ago, Jesus gathered together his friends and took a cup of wine, blessed it, and shared it with them. We do that now, praying that even as Jesus was able to go forward from that night with the strength and support he gained from you, his God, and from his friends, we might be able to do the same. We pray that by sharing in this common cup, we know the power of his presence in our midst and might open our hearts to one another. Bless us now, for the days and life ahead of us.

OUR FATHER...

SHARING OF THE CUP

CLOSING

Leader: We have imagined, for just a short time, what it might be like if the bombs had been dropped, if nuclear war had happened. We imagined, for just a short time, what it might have been like trying to maintain faith and hope in a situation as tragic and horrendous as that survival.

If it is true that even in that situation of unspeakable despair, we would be able to offer words to each other that might enable our survival, how much more likely is it that today, in these real and present days of imminent crisis, we might be able to offer such words of *faith, hope,* and *courage* that could PREVENT such destruction from ever happening.

With such words as we have given each other —
With such words as God has given us —
Let us go in peace to love and serve the people of our God.

Share a sign of peace.

Belonging/Naming

Participants can be seated in a circle. Each participant takes time to state his or her full name and provide some background about these names. The leader begins. Some history about your name might include: who named you and why, what are your nicknames, what does your first name mean, what nationality are you, was your last name ever changed, do you like your name, etc. Go around the circle taking turns. You will be delighted in your discovery of something unique about each of the people in your circle.

SONG

Celebrate being named and called as a unique person by joining in singing an appropriate song for your group, like:

- *"Anthem," by Tom Conry*

- *"Paint My Life," by John Michael Talbot*

- *"Sister," by Cris Williamson (women's gathering)*

- *Closing Song: "We Are the World," from USA for Africa*

READING

I THANK YOU FOR THOSE THINGS
THAT ARE YET POSSIBLE

O God of timelessness
   and time,
I thank you for my time
and for those things that are yet possible
   and precious in it:
      daybreak and beginning again,
         midnight and the touch of angels,
            the taming of demons in the dance of dreams;
a word of forgiveness,
   and sometimes a song,
for my breathing...my life.

Thank you
for the honesty which makes friends
   and makes laughter;
for fierce gentleness
   which dares to speak the truth in love
      and tugs me to join the long march toward peace;
for the sudden gusts of grace
   which rise unexpectedly in my wending from dawn to dawn;
for children unabashed,
   wind rippling a rain puddle,
      a mockingbird in the darkness,
         a colleague and a cup of coffee;
for all the mysteries of loving,
   of my body next to another's body;
for music and silence,
   for wrens and Orion,
      for everything that moves me to tears,
         to touching,
            to dreams,
               to prayers;
for my longing...my life.

Thank you
for work
    which engages me in an internal debate
        between right and reward
    and stretches me toward responsibility
        to those who pay for my work,
            and those who cannot pay
                because they have no work;
for justice
    which repairs the devastations of poverty;
for liberty
    which extends to the captives of violence;
for healing
    which binds up the broken bodied
        and the broken hearted;
for bread broken
    for all the hungry of the earth;
for good news
    of love which is stronger than death;
and for peace
    for all to sit under fig trees
        and not be afraid;
for my calling... my life.

Thank you
for the sharp senses
    of the timeless stirring in my time,
        and your praise in my heart;
for the undeniable awareness, quick as now,
    that the need of you
        is the truth of me,
    and your presence with me
        is the truth of you,
    which sets me free
        for others, for joy, and for you;
for your grace... my life... forever.

                  — From *Guerrillas of Grace,*
                  by Ted Loder, pp. 42–43

RITUAL ACTION

Standing in an open circle or a circle joining hands or arms, bring to the circle those friends, special people, contemporary challenging people, whom you would like to remember. For example:

- I bring to our circle the special Dorothys in my life:

      Dorothy Day
      Dorothy Kazel
      and my good friend Dorothy _____ .

- The leader sounds a small chime, a triangle, or a bell, after which all respond aloud: "Welcome to our circle!" This continues until all have had an opportunity to express names.

Hope in Winter

"I Long for You," by the Dameans, or other songs of hope or need.

OPENING PRAYER

All: We pray to you,
O promised One,
and ask what hope have you to give us
when heaviness weighs on us like a blanket
and our hearts can find small cause for joy?
What promise can you make
that would restore our spirit?
We see need on every side,
hear questions without answers,
feel hunger with no food that satisfies.
How long, O God,
before you come?
How long before you once more work wonders
in our hearts and land?
We have need of you.
We go blind for lack of hope.
Come quickly,
Promise of our God.

ANTIPHONAL PRAYER

Left: Praise to you for summer, fall, and spring.
But faith reserves the right to wonder
when chill of winter invades our bones.

Right: Where are you when a sign is asked
and none is given,
and barrenness in earth and soul
is all we know?

Left: Enough of it! We've had enough
of grey and cold and emptiness.
Life wears heavily and joy becomes a victim
in the winter of our hearts.

Right: What good is death if Easter never comes,
if any sign of risen life is only in our memory
and promises are all past due?

Left: Revive. Restore. Lift up our hearts
and, with them, all creation.
Breathe upon your world and warm us all.

Right: What word have you for those who wait,
for those who long like deer for running streams,
like infants for their mothers' breasts,
who yearn like birds for flight?
What word have you for us who wait?

READING

FOR THOSE IN A WINTRY SEASON

Winter sleeps heavily in the spirit;
Eyes are windows to the glacial land;
Fog curls into the valleys of decision;
No way forward: Where is God
In the winter of the soul?

Faces smile and flash content
But like sparkling snow cover

The dirty slush of despair.
In silhouetted barren branches;
Nothing growing, nothing resting...emptiness.

Where is God in the winter of the soul?
Will icelogged rivers of love flow again;
Will warmth burn away the cold?
Believing in things unseen:
Hope
    is the winter name of God...

                         —Sally Dyck

OPPORTUNITY FOR SHARING AND PRAYER

CLOSING PRAYER

We pray in thanks for those with hope around us,
for eyes to see the ever-present hint of spring within our soul.
Thanks be to you for the gentle, persistent power of your love
that asserts itself within us,
and will not be denied until it buds, then bursts, full-flower.
We praise you for your patience
with our blindness and our short-lived memories,
and stand dumbfounded that you accept us all and all within us
and dare to take delight in us.
This alone is cause for hope—
to know your ease with our dis-ease of self.
We trust that what you know and love of us
gives peace today and future promise.
Amen.

Celebrate Women

Leader: Let us begin our celebration together
             by worshipping God,
             our Mother and Father,
             the Ground of our being,
             the Source of our life,
             the Spirit who sets us free.

All: In memory of all the women
             who have sung praise to God
             before we were born
             and in union with all women living today,
             we join to praise the Spirit of God in our midst.

Leader: To worship is to open our beings
             to the power of God's truth and love.
             To worship is to heighten our awareness
             of the core of our existence,
             the meaning of life.

All: Let us celebrate with joy
             in the hope that our awareness and openness
             will bear the fruit of increased union
             with God's Spirit in each of us.

READING

LITANY OF NAMING

Let us begin by remembering the stories of our foremothers and praying that their courage to name, claim, and move with their visions may be shared by women and men of our time and spark us to be *women moving church.*

We come here as daughters and sons of the women in our own families who have gone before us and have given us life. Let us share the names of these women now as we name ourselves as their descendants.

Individuals each read one phrase.

Mothers in our families, you have named us and have given us life, our mothers, move here with us.

Eve and Lilith, Mothers of Life, you claimed your own power by reaching for knowledge and found it was good, Eve and Lilith, move here with us.

Ruth and Naomi, your devoted love for one another renewed your faith in the working of the divine, Ruth and Naomi, move here with us.

Mary, you listened, pondered, and knew that you had been chosen to give birth to Jesus, one who is Truth and Life, Mary, move here with us.

Mary Magdalene, you were the disciple to the disciples, sharing with them the first news of the resurrection, Mary Magdalene, move here with us.

Catherine of Siena, you reconciled warring factions of state and church and we name you Doctor of our Church, Catherine of Siena, move here with us.

Kateri Tekakwitha, Lily of the Mohawks, you showed the form of faith incarnated in the Native Americas of our land, and showed how suffering for that faith brings life, Kateri Tekakwitha, move here with us.

Mother Jones, you spoke out with authority opposing the injustices against women, men, and children in the workplace, Mother Jones and all working women, move here with us.

Matilda Joslyn Gage, you lost your rightful place in history even in women's stories, because you too clearly named and focused the central women's issues: women's oppression by the church, the state, the capitalists, and the home, Matilda Joslyn Gage, move here with us.

Rosa Parks, you sparked the Civil Rights movement in the South by refusing to give your seat to a white man and move to the back of the bus, Rosa Parks, move here with us.

Dolores Huerta, with Cesar Chavez you led the United Farm Workers and their supporters toward the Promised Land of a just wage and humane working conditions, Dolores Huerta, move here with us.

Ita Ford, Maura Clark, Dorothy Kazel, Jean Donovan, you risked your lives providing the basic needs of the poor of El Salvador in their struggle for human rights, Ita, Maura, Dorothy, Jean, move here with us.

Babies born in 198–, to you is given the challenge of a world bursting with possibilities for justice. In you we place dreams for peace and harmony, visions of equality and transformation, be, move here with us.

— Diann Neu, WATER Publications

Go around your circle remembering your genealogies and the foremothers in your own families.

PRAYER

Leader: Spirit of God,
you are the life-giving Spirit who sets us free.
You are both promise and uncertainty,
poverty and hope, comfort and challenge.
Inspire us with courage to proclaim the truth
and strength to work for justice and peace.
Waken in us a spirit of joy
that we may celebrate all that is good and human,
and, especially today, all that is woman.
To the women whose names we have just spoken,
to all the special women in our lives,
and to each person here,
send your Spirit, O God,

to make us whole,
to make us know that you have created us in your image,
and that you are our Mother and Father,
our sister and brother,
our friend.

All: Amen.

BLESSING AND EMPOWERMENT

Salt symbolizes the salt of the earth, power, source of strength. Give each person a small container of salt.

In blessing our foreheads,
we claim the power of reason,
to know that path that leads to the fulfillment
of our hopes for a liberated humankind.

In blessing our eyes,
we claim the power of vision,
to see clearly the forces of life and death in our midst.

In blessing our ears,
we claim the power to hear the Spirit of God
as She speaks to us within.

In blessing our lips,
we claim the power to speak the truth about our experience;
we claim power to name ourselves and our God.

In blessing our hands,
we claim our powers as creators of a new humanity
liberated from fear, ignorance, and oppression.

In blessing our feet,
we claim the power to walk the paths of our courageous foremothers
and to forge new paths where they are needed.

In blessing each other,
we claim the creative power that rests collectively
in our shared struggle as women and men.
We choose to extend this power in service to a world in need.

May our lives be blessings to each other.
Amen.

—Prayer and Blessing taken from
25th Anniversary of Ellen Rufft, CDP,
Pittsburgh, Pa.

SONG

SISTER

Born of the earth, a child of God
Just one among family.
And you can count on me to share the load
And I will always help you
Hold your burdens, and I will be the one
Lean on me, I am your sister.
Believe on me, I am your friend.
Lean on me, I am your sister.
Believe on me, I am your friend.

I will fold you in my arms like a white-winged dove.
Shine in your soul, your spirit is crying.

—Cris Williamson

Commissioning

PREPARATION

This service can be used for teachers at the beginning of school year, for persons being commissioned, or at the beginning of a new year for a committee. Adjust the service to meet your needs.

A table or altar is needed. Loaves of bread (use a variety) will later be placed on the table.

INVITATION TO PRAYER

Gather participants for prayer and an explanation of the commissioning service.

INTRODUCTION

The Beatitudes are for people who have their hearts set on having the Reign of God come about. Beatitudes are a way of life designed for those who want their lives to be a blessing. Beatitude people are searching people. They have this working with God on their minds and they can't rest until the world is right and just and equitable for all. They urge us out of the comfortable and the ordinary. They invite us to risk in our daily living and meet the holy in the unsettling questions of the day. They tell us that God is forever in our midst if we bless the world with Beatitude-living. The Beatitudes are values that come straight from the mind of Christ. Translated into simple language, Jesus could have said something like this:

- Blessed are those who are convinced of their basic dependency on God, whose lives are emptied of all that doesn't matter, those for whom the riches of this world just aren't that important.

  The Reign of heaven is theirs.

- Blessed are those who know that all they are is gift from God, and so they can be content with their greatness and their smallness, knowing themselves and being true to themselves.

  For they shall have the earth for their heritage.

- Blessed are those who wear compassion like a garment, those who have learned how to find themselves by losing themselves in another's sorrow.

  For they too shall receive comfort.

- Blessed are those who are hungry for goodness, those who never get enough of God and truth and righteousness.

  For they shall be satisfied.

- Blessed are the merciful, those who remember how much has been forgiven them, and are able to extend this forgiveness into the lives of others.

  For they too shall receive God's mercy.

- Blessed are those whose hearts are free and simple, those who have smashed all false images and are seeking honestly for truth.

  For they shall see God.

- Blessed are the creators of peace, those who build roads that unite rather than walls that divide, those who bless the world with the healing power of their presence.

  For they shall be called children of God.

- Blessed are those whose love has been tried, like gold, in the furnace and found to be precious, genuine, and lasting, those who have lived their belief out loud, no matter what the cost or pain.

For theirs is the kingdom of heaven.

— From *Seasons of Your Heart,*
by Macrina Wiederkehr, OSB, p. 78

RITUAL

As each beatitude above is read, one person from the group stands, raises a loaf of fresh bread and slowly carries it to a central table (altar). As each walks forward, all sing a refrain, for example, the refrain from "Bread for the Hungry," by Joe Wise. Then the second beatitude is read, and so on.

HOMILY

A leader is needed in order to speak about what this event symbolizes. Make the connection with being called to be Beatitude-people for this group. Make it as personalized as possible. This can be a short homily or dialogue-sharing.

REFLECTION

After the person speaks, or the dialogue-sharing takes place, pause for a few moments of silence.

RITUAL

One person at a time is called forward by name. Depending on the size of the group, the leader gives each person one of the loaves of bread or a piece of one. The leader expresses a blessing to each person, for example, "Go forth and be bread for the hungry," or a similar expression. Soft music can be playing in the background.

CONCLUSION

Pray together:

Compassionate God,
we are here to give ourselves to you and to your people.

It is through what we are and do that others will come to know you.
We are here to bring peace to a broken people,
and healing to those in need.
We are here to witness to the world,
that we live in response to a desperate society
seeking truth, equality, and freedom.

Parent of the poor and oppressed, we ask for your help.
You have shown us how to be faithful in the midst of persecution.
You have taught us to stand firm in the pain
that we experience in our broken world.
Teach us to become sight for the blind,
ears for those who are deaf to hear your Word,
and hands for those who refuse to work
at building the Reign of God.
We pray all this in your name and for your honor and glory.

Prayer to the Four Winds

This prayer, expressive of Native American spirituality, is perhaps best led by one person. She or he invites the gathering to face the North and, with arms outstretched, proclaims the prayer, allowing a brief pause before inviting the group to turn and face each new direction. The prayer closes with all facing the North again, with arms either outstretched or down at sides.

THE NORTH

We greet you, Spirit of the North.
You are the cold, biting wind that blows across our land,
that strips the earth of all that is dead and decayed,
that robs us of the false securities, so easily blown away.

Teach us to plant our feet securely on the earth
and to see things as they really are,
that the coming of your Spirit may find us standing firm in integrity.

It is your Spirit whose winds bring the snows of winter,
with their fury and their solitude.
It is your Spirit who blankets the earth for sleep.

Teach us, Spirit of the North, in the solitude of winter,
to wait in darkness with the sleeping earth,
believing that we, like the earth,
already hold within ourselves the seeds of new life.

THE EAST

Turn toward the East.

We greet you, O Spirit of the East.
You usher in the dawn on your breeze;
you stretch forth your fingers and paint our skies.

Awaken in us with each day,
new hopes, new dreams of colors,
love and joys never before imagined.

Fill our bodies with your breath; invigorate us.
Carry us to the farthest mountains and beyond.

In-spirit us that we might reach out to you boldly
to grasp the miracles that are given birth with each new dawn.

THE SOUTH

Turn toward the South.

We greet you, Spirit of the South.
You bring the winds of summer
and breathe on us the warmth of the sun
to soothe and heal our bodies and our spirits.

You thaw and soften the coldness of our world;
you nudge the seedlings to break through the soil to light.

Quicken us, draw us by the urgings of your warm breath
to break through the soil of our own barrenness and fear.

Drive our roots deep into the earth
and stretch our branches full out into the sky.

Teach us to hold sacred the memory of the spring rains
that we might have the strength to withstand the heat of the day,
and not become parched and narrow in our love.

Lead us to accept fatigue with resignation,
knowing that life is not to be rushed,

that there is no flower of the field
that grows from seed to blossom in a single day.

THE WEST

Turn toward the West

We greet you, Spirit of the West.
You cool our hot and tired bodies,
refresh and bring laughter to our hearts.
It is you who usher in the setting sun.

It is by your power that the sun hangs suspended for endless moments
before you catch it with your breath and carry it off into the night.

Guide our steps at end of day; keep us safe from evil.
Fill us with your peace as you enfold us with your great mystery of night
that we might rest securely in your arms
until morning calls us forth again.

THE EARTH

Turn toward the North.

We greet you, Great Spirit of the Earth.
It was from you we came as from a Mother;
you nourish us still and give us shelter.

Teach us to walk softly on your lands,
to use with care your gifts,
to love with tenderness all our brothers and sisters
who have been born of your goodness.

And when the day comes that you call us back to yourself,
help us to return to you as a friend,
to find ourselves embraced, encircled, enfolded in your arms.

Nourishment/Growth

PREPARATION

If possible have participants seated in a circle (or a double circle). At one end of the circle, where all can see, have a low table with a large container of soil, a wicker basket of wheat berry seeds (available at health food stores), and possibly an earth-tone cloth on the table. The leader should sit near the basket of seeds.

MUSIC AND OPENING PRAYER

Soft music can be playing for a few minutes. The reading begins after listening to the music, which will help focus people for prayer. The music can continue during the reading. If there are musicians in your group, flute or violin music would be appropriate. Otherwise, use soft instrumental music from a tape or record.

READING

I WONDER IF THE GROUND HAS ANYTHING TO SAY?

The occasion for the speech was an Indian council in the Valley of Walla Walla in 1855. Young Chief of the Cayuses gave this speech before being forced to sign away the land.

I wonder if the ground has anything to say? I wonder if the ground is listening to what is said? I wonder if the ground will come alive...? I hear what the ground says. The ground says, It is the Great Spirit that placed me here. The Great Spirit tells me to take care of the Indians, to feed them aright. The Great Spirit appointed the roots to feed the Indians on. The water says the same thing. The Great Spirit directs me, Feed the Indians well. The grass says the same thing, Feed the Indians well. The ground, water, and grass say, The Great Spirit has given us our names. We have these names and hold these names. The ground says, The Great Spirit has placed me here to produce all that grows on me, trees and fruits. . . . The ground says, It was from me human beings were made. The Great Spirit, in placing people on the earth, desired them to take good care of the ground and to do each other no harm. . . .

— Adapted from Lawrence Kip, *The Indian Council in the Valley of the Walla Walla*

REFLECTION

And Jesus said, "Unless a grain of wheat falls to the ground and dies, it shall not have life. . . . "

The ground is sacred, both to the Indians and to people today who treasure the land as a holy gift from God. Wheat berry seeds symbolize the nourishment we receive from Mother Earth. Our Native American sisters and brothers depended on the growth of these seeds for their livelihood. Farmers today also depend on their growth.

Take some seeds from the basket and let them fall from your hand to the basket, repeating this movement several times.

Our livelihood depends more on cooperation, collaboration, and sharing of resources and talents than on competition. In the past few months or years, what experiences, events, or people have been sources of nourishment in our lives?

Take time to share these experiences. The leader might begin. As the sharing comes to an end, begin reflective background music. After a few moments the leader invites all to pray aloud for those who have provided nourishment for us today. After each prayer all respond:

"For giving us life, we thank you!"

CONCLUDING PRAYER

Pray together:

- Blessed are you, strong and faithful God.
  all your works, the height and the depth,
  echo the silent music of your praise.

  In the beginning your Word summoned light:
  night withdrew, and creation dawned.
  As ages passed unseen,
  waters gathered on the face of the earth
  and life appeared.

- How wonderful the works of your hands, O Lord!
  As a mother tenderly gathers her children,
  you embraced a people as your own
  and filled them with longing
  for a peace that would last
  and for justice that would never fail.

  Through countless generations
  your people hungered for the bread of freedom.
  From them you raised up Jesus, the living bread,
  in whom ancient hungers were satisfied.

- When the times had at last grown full
  and the earth had ripened in abundance,
  you created in your image humankind,
  the crown of all creation.

  You gave us breath and speech,
  that all the living
  might find a voice to sing your praise.
  So now, with all the powers of heaven and earth,
  we chant the ageless hymn of your glory:

Sung:

- Holy, holy, holy Lord, God of power and might,
  Heaven and earth are full of your glory.

Hosanna in the highest!
Blessed is he who comes in the name of the Lord.
Hosanna in the highest!

—From "A New Eucharistic Prayer," by
John Page, *America,* February 16, 1985

*As all leave the place of worship, take some of the wheat berry seeds
and return them to the earth.*

Creating a New World Order

INVITATION TO PRAYER

Leader: Let our prayer arise before you.

All: And may your grace descend upon the world.

Leader: Accept our prayers with all who are praising you this very moment.

All: And send your spirit to renew the face of the earth.

Leader: Give to us, God, eyes for seeing.

All: And ears to hear your word.

READING

Julia Esquivel, an exiled Guatemalan poet, mourns her beloved country. Light a candle as a sign that we accompany the people of Guatemala in their struggle for liberation. The Spanish sections can be read by one person. Slides are optional for this reading.

It isn't the noise in the streets
that keeps us from resting, my friend,
nor is it the shouts of the young people
coming out drunk from "St. Paul's" bar,
nor is it the tumult of those who pass by
excitedly on their way to the mountains.

There is something here within us
which doesn't let us sleep,
which doesn't let us rest,
which doesn't stop pounding deep inside,
it is the silent, warm weeping
of Indian women without their husbands,
it is the sad gaze of the children
fixed there beyond memory
in the very pupil of our eyes which during sleep,
though closed, keep watch
with each contraction of the heart,
in every awakening...

What keeps us from sleeping is that
they have threatened us with Resurrection!

[Echo: *Nos han amenazado de resurrección*]

Because we have felt their inert bodies
and their souls penetrated ours doubly fortified.
Because in this marathon of Hope,
there are always others to relieve us
in bearing the courage necessary
to arrive at the goal which lies beyond death.

They have threatened us with Resurrection

[Echo: *Nos han amenazado de resurrección*]

because they are more alive than ever before,
because they transform our agonies,
and fertilize our struggle,
because they pick us up when we fall,
and gird us like giants
before the fear of those demented gorillas.

They have threatened us with Resurrection

[Echo: *Nos han amenazado de resurrección*]

because they do not know life (poor things!).

This is the whirlwind which does not let us sleep,

the reason why asleep, we keep watch,
and awake, we dream.

No, it's not the street noises,
nor the shouts from the drunks in "St. Paul's" bar,
nor the noise from the fans at the ball park.
It is the internal cyclone of a kaleidoscopic struggle
which will heal the wound of the quetzal
fallen in Ixcan.
It is the earthquake soon to come that
will shake the world
and put everything in its place...

Acompáñanos	Accompany us then
en esta vigilia	on this vigil
y sabrás	and you will know
lo que es soñar!	what it is to dream!
Sabrás entonces	You will then know
lo maravilloso que es	how marvelous it is
vivir amenazado	to live
de Resurrección!	threatened with Resurrection!
Soñar despierto,	To dream awake,
velar dormido,	to keep watch asleep,
vivir muriendo	to live while dying
y saberse	and to already know oneself
ya resucitado!	resurrected!

— Julia Esquivel, "They Have Threatened
Us with Resurrection"; "[Echoes]," by Diann
L. Neu, in *Women Church Celebrations*

PSALM 146

All: Yahweh protects the stranger
and gives justice to the oppressed.

Leader: Praise Yahweh, my soul!
I mean to praise Yahweh all my life.
I mean to sing to my God as long as I live.

All: Yahweh protects the stranger
and gives justice to the oppressed.

Leader: Yahweh, forever faithful,
gives justice to those denied it,
gives food to the hungry,
gives liberty to prisoners.

All: Yahweh protects the stranger
and gives justice to the oppressed.

Leader: Yahweh loves the virtuous, and frustrates the wicked.
Yahweh reigns forever, your God Zion, from age to age.

All: Yahweh protects the stranger
and gives justice to the oppressed.

— Bob Hoover, "Psalm 146,"
in *Central America Reflections*

PRAYER RESPONSE

Invite prayer responses from individuals.

CLOSING PRAYER

May God grant us visions of truth,
graces to preserve,
and integrity in purpose and action
as we pursue living as good and faithful stewards.
May people be free from oppression
and may the new world order be focused on the sharing of the goods
given to us by our loving God.

May we live together praising God's holy name
and working together for the coming of this new world order.
Amen.

SONG

*"City of God," by Dan Schutte, SJ,
or "Peace Prayer," by John Foley, SJ.*

Peace Pentecost

A table with five candles placed on it. Space the candles so there is room later in the service to place symbols near each candle.

INTRODUCTION

Leader: Peace Pentecost is a time to take our prayers for peace to unlikely places. On this day Christians beseech the Holy Spirit in government buildings, on railroad tracks, and at nuclear weapons facilities. At all these places, in so many cities, the prayer lifted heavenward is one that has been raised up since the first Pentecost: "Come Holy Spirit." This Pentecost we again join with our sisters and brothers all over the world and in particular with those in Washington, D.C., where so many decisions are made — some of those decisions that have led to so much violence and injustice for people in this country and all over the world.

In the midst of so much violence and death, we are tempted to falter in our hope. In such a time, our coming together today is an opportunity for revival and a chance to be refreshed and renewed in our struggle for justice, peace, and freedom.

— "In the Company of the Faithful," by
Vincent Harding, in *Sojourners,* May 1985

89

MUSIC

"Renew the Earth," by Marcie Silvestro (from the album/tape "Circling Free"), or another appropriate song.

READINGS

Read these reflections or others you have about contemporary peace-makers. As each is read, light a candle and remember their spirit and their beliefs that continue to live on in our lives.

> *Dietrich Bonhoeffer: a small German symbol, e.g., a flag*
> *Barbara Deming: a metal bar (symbolizing bars of a jail)*
> *Martin Luther King, Jr.: his picture or a peace symbol*
> *Thomas Merton: one of his books*
> *Dorothy Day: a symbol of women or a copy of the* Catholic Worker

As each candle is lit, place the symbol for each reading on the table by the candle. Sound a drum or chimes as each name is proclaimed.

DIETRICH BONHOEFFER

And then in this time there are witnesses who are very fitting for just this American hour, like Bonhoeffer, like the Confessing Church of Germany. You taught us that the time comes again and again in Christian faith when Christian people must go against their own government in order to go for life. Dietrich Bonhoeffer, help us to know to do that without self-righteousness, without fear, without recrimination, and, as you have learned, without being overwhelmed by the temptation to violence. In a time when our own government is moving against the compassion of God's love for the world, teach us how to speak and live truth, no matter what the cost. Teach us how to love America and its people so much that we will risk our lives in the struggle for transformation, for the new city, for the new land. Thank you.

BARBARA DEMING

There are so many. As the writer says, "Tongue can hardly name them." Barbara Deming — sure, she's here. I don't understand all of Barbara Deming. I don't understand how she put together so many parts of her life. But I know that Barbara was in that Albany, Georgia, jail with black people and white people, just calling upon Jesus in her own marvelously agnostic way. And I want Barbara Deming to know that I know that they are here, and that we need their courage; and that some of us need to know how to be a woman — how to be woman-tough, how to be woman-loving, how to be woman-compassionate, how to be woman-courageous, how to be woman. I think Barbara knows something about that.

MARTIN LUTHER KING, JR.

Do you see, do you sense, do you feel Martin here? Thank God for Martin Luther King, Jr. Let him teach us whatever he will. Let him teach us how to choose, how to make hard choices for peace and freedom, even as he did, against the fears of his parents and his friends. Let him teach us how to choose even against the ways of his tribe. Let him teach us how he got on the case for the poor, and once that scent was in his nostrils, how he was never to be turned aside from his total conviction that the poor must find life and power in our society. Martin, help us.

THOMAS MERTON

And how can we come to this gathering and not know that brother Tom Merton is right here, with his old, beat-up, longshoreman's wool cap on, looking like anything but a monk, but being an ultimate servant of God. Stand with us, Tom. Teach us how in the strangest, most isolated places you can let the pain of the world come into you, how you can feel black people in the monastery in Kentucky. How you can feel poor people, how you can feel them so much that you have no peace in your peaceful setting. Teach us, Tom, how to live in peace out of peace, how to stand in that paradox — and write poetry!

DOROTHY DAY

Dorothy Day, thank you for being with us, you magnificent old curmudgeon! You beautiful, strong, determined woman, you old lover of the poor, thank you for being here. Teach us how to live for the poor. Teach us how to make the poor the center of our concerns, Dorothy. And don't let us excuse ourselves with anything about being women, about not being married, about being old, about anything. Teach us, Dorothy!

— "In the Company of the Faithful," by
Vincent Harding, in *Sojourners*, May 1985

SHARED PRAYER

Invite all to name contemporary people who are peacemakers in their personal lives. Participants can mention names and share why they are important.

MUSIC

A song can be played here, for example, "Choose Life," by Gregory Norbet, OSB.

CONCLUDING PRAYER

PEACEMAKERS PRAYER

O God of peace,
sparkle our staleness with your hope,
invade the depth of our being with new courage,
defeat us in your love.

Grant that our lives may be:
surprising in forgiveness and healing,
abounding in joy and laughter,
daring in deeds and dreams of justice.

May we be do-ers, makers, pray-ers of peace
in memory of Christ Jesus. Amen.

—From the Dedication Liturgy of
Peacemakers Chapel, Walsh College,
Canton, Ohio, January 15, 1984

Transforming Spirit

CALL TO PRAYER

Leader: Come to our aid, Spirit of power.

All: Spirit who moves among us, strengthen us, we pray.

Leader: Come to us, Spirit of compassion.

All: Spirit who transforms the face of the earth,
turn our hearts to the needs of the poor.

Leader: Spirit of the Living One, stay with us.

All: Rouse us from our sleep and bring forth life in us.
Let it rise up, full-term, image and apple of your eye.

SONG

"Send Us Your Spirit," by David Haas, or another appropriate song.

READING

Transforming Womb of God,
Conceive in us.
Create anew life:
     Faith, the confidence to bear,
     Hope, continuously expectant,
     Love, the true beginning.

Break forth your living water, O birthing-Spirit;
Streaming grace upon us,
Waters from your belly;
Cleansing us, causing us to be whole;
Giving us this living water,
Overflowing our cup,
Thirsting no more;
Longing for your welling pool,
Healing as the juices of crushed aloe.
Breaking waters, life-giving Spirit,
Trusting in your presence through the rushing rapids.

Kind hands upon your full belly;
Expecting the yet unseen,
Anticipating the given moment,
Moving with your birthing rhythms;
Breathing with the pain.
Body suffering, shedding blood.
Dying into life from the dark
Night of the uniting womb.
Signs of new beginnings
Casting forth into light.
Meeting of the Creator and newly born;
A joyful morning! A jubilee!
First-born, your name upon us;
Our name engraved upon your palm.

Hearing our nightly crying —
     the sick, the brokenhearted, the bound,
     the foolish, the weak, the unlovely —
Offering your loving breast, our banquet table,
Warm milk of sustenance
Given freely, freely flowing, flowing in abundance.

Nurturing the Nurturer: our mission
In memory of your body and your blood,
Returning our cup to the thirsty;
Working together, laborers of the Body,
Lovers in our service.

Your whole creation, our field;
Your wisdom, our teacher;
Your inspiration, our vision;
Your presence, our altar.

Transforming Womb of God,
Conceive in us.
Create anew life:
      Faith, the confidence to bear,
      Hope, continuously expectant,
      Love, the true beginning.

> —From "Faith and Imagination: The Holy
> Spirit and the Ministry of the Church,"
> by Sally Dyck

OPPORTUNITY FOR PRAYER OR SHARED REFLECTION

*After some time of quiet, the leader might invite those gathered to repeat
the line or phrase of the reading that spoke to them and share something
of the insight gained.*

*After all have finished, the leader gathers together the "words" that
have been spoken by asking people simply to repeat the line or phrase
shared earlier and then inviting people to join in the closing prayer that
follows.*

PRAYER

All: We give you thanks, Spirit of wisdom,
            for you speak to us in ways
            that often surprise us.
            You uncover truths that
            we had kept hidden from ourselves
            and support us in tasks we fear to undertake alone.

            We give thanks
            for your invitations
            to growth and intimacy and fullness of life,
            and for the comfort you extend
            in our often uphill struggle
            to be faithful.

Inspire us. Encourage us.
Fill us with enthusiasm
for the mission of your Church.
"Transforming Womb of God,
Conceive in us.
We ask you, create life anew:
    Faith, the confidence to bear,
    Hope, continuously expectant,
    Love, the true beginning."

CLOSING SONG

"Song of the Soul," by Cris Williamson, or another song of fullness of life.

The following four services are a set. Each service is focused on one direction: South, North, East, or West, and each of these earth-directions is related to a symbol.

South — Fire
North — Earth
East — Air
West — Water

Fire (South)

Have a bag of clothes representing poor bag people, a candle, pictures or newspaper articles, red, orange, and yellow sashes or cloths. Some of these items could be placed on a table in the room near a wall that faces south. If possible, sit near a fireplace in the room.

CALL TO PRAYER

Presider:	Loving God, come to our assistance.
All:	God, make haste to help us.
Presider:	Let justice inflame our hearts,
All:	and integrity like a torch of love.
Presider:	Rise, Eternal Flame, raise your hand, do not forget the poor.
All:	You yourself have seen the distress and grief, you watch and take them into your hands.
Presider:	Eternal Flame, you listen to the wants of the humble, you bring strength to their hearts.
All:	You grant them a hearing, judging in favor of the orphaned and the exploited

so that earthborn women and men
may strike fear no longer.

DEATH NOTICE

Of the 120 million children born in 1979, the year of the child,
more than 16 million have experienced hunger.
Today, November 13, 1981, on the first day of Peace Week,

15,000 human beings

are dying of hunger.
And on this day the rest of us are spending 1.4 billion dollars
for military weapons.
We are grieving...

— From *Not Just Yes and Amen,* by Dorothee
Soelle and Fulbert Steffensky, p. 14

READING

Reader 1:   O God, you who love all your children,
the oppressed, the oppressors,
and those who sit on the sidelines.
We believe that you will raise up the oppressed,
bring down the oppressors,
and bring to their feet
those who sit by in apathy or ignorance.
But how long, O God, will you wait to bring justice?
How long, O God?

Reader 2:   We would remember
those who are oppressed in Central America
and countries of strife throughout the world.
Our prayers are lifted for those who have died,
those who have been wounded or maimed,
those who are imprisoned or tortured,
those who face threats of violence,
and those whose loved ones
have been seared by violence.

Reader 3: We would remember the oppressors,
those persons who have mistaken, O God,
your promise of bountiful life —
mistaken this promise to mean
that they are due all the good things of this world —
no matter the costs for others.

Reader 1: O God,
may the scales fall from the eyes of the oppressors
and from their hearts.
May they see the destruction they wreak
on themselves,
their neighbors,
and all our posterity.
May their blind eyes be open to see,
may they turn in repentance,
and may they know your forgiveness.

Reader 2: We would remember the peacemakers —
those who risk their lives,
their health,
and their sanity
in the desperate struggle
to bring justice and reconciliation.
May they have clarity of vision,
tenacity of conviction,
and compassion for their enemies.

Reader 3: We would pray for those
who see themselves as uninvolved,
who, like us Americans,
ignored rape, torture, and death in Central America
until it happened to our own sisters and brothers.
Forgive us, O God!

Reader 1: O how long,
O God, until you bring peace in Central America.
We pray that you would enliven our prayers,
open our eyes,
and strengthen our actions

so that your peace, your joy, and your glory
might be made known to all humanity,
especially to the people of Central America.

All: Amen.

— Adapted from the prayer by Bob Hoover,
in *Central American Reflections*

RESPONSE

Song "Bread for the Hungry," by Joe Wise, taken from the album Song
for the Journey, *1979.*

REFLECTIVE READING

*Before the reader begins the reflection below, invite all to stand and face
the south. Use fire as a focus, for example, light some candles or light a
fire in a fireplace, and continue reading "The South."*

THE SOUTH

As the North corresponds to midnight and winter, so the South reminds
us of noon and summer. The South is characterized by heat, fire, and
energy. Its colors are those of fire: red, orange, and yellow. Since it
requires great endurance to withstand the energy and fiery spirit of the
South, this direction symbolizes strength of will.

Take time apart to reflect on these questions:

- When we say that God's love is especially attentive to the poor
  or that it is "preferential," we mean that it is a love whose depth
  and vigor is most dramatic among the poor. In what ways have I
  witnessed "preferential" love for the poor?

- How do I promote peace and love for the poor in my own personal
  goals and in my life?

FAITH SHARING

All return to share a "one-liner" that begins: "A new insight or image that came to me was..."

CLOSING PRAYER

Father of the Poor.
Mother of Mercy.
God of all consolation!
Your silence makes a mockery of your name.
Come, God of Justice.
Too much suffering, too many deaths.
You have waited long enough!
Strike quickly in our world and today in our hearts.

Earth (North)

Use soil and wildflowers. Have a candle for each person: light it from a central candle before each person shares. When all are invited to face the North, have these earth symbols near the North. If the service takes place outdoors, soil can be used creatively, reminding people of the earth that we stand on. Drop soil to the earth as all are invited to face the North.

CALL TO PRAYER

Presider: Creator God, come to our assistance.

All: God, make haste to help us.

Presider: Let justice shine like the light.

All: And integrity like an unfailing beam.

Presider: Rise, God of Light, raise your hand,
do not forget the poor.

All: You yourself have seen the distress and grief;
you watch and take them into your hands.

Presider: Yahweh, you listen to the wants of the humble,
you bring strength to their hearts.

All: Holy One, you grant them a hearing,
          judging in favor of the orphaned and the exploited,
          so that earthborn women and men
          may strike fear no longer.

READING

THE FOUR ELEMENTS

I pulled the tip of my finger
Out of the keyhole,
And you came in, my ghost,
Bringing so much bouillabaisse
Smelled from the upper room
But left downstairs unsipped.

We lifted the ladle a million times,
Till gasping for thirst and air
I opened the window and released the sea
Tapping and taunting on the panes.

It came in full flood on you and me
Now merged to a bloated boat
Filled with fluid fish,
And we launched into a thirsty sea
Of two times a million two of a kind
Sea creatures quite as drunk as we.

In forty days and forty nights
We and the waters tired
And collapsed into a small fire bird
Tapping and taunting on dry mountain ground.

—From *Views from the Intersection: Poems and
Meditations,* by Virginia Ramey Mollenkott
and Catherine Barry, p. 65

MEDITATION

After "forty days and forty nights" — the time period associated in
the Bible with spiritual preparation, self-knowledge, and transformation — the whole watery self-exploration experience is transformed into

a phoenix, a "small fire bird/Tapping and taunting on the dry mountain ground." The phoenix, or fire bird, is a famous symbol of death and resurrection, since it periodically immolates itself and then is reborn out of its own ashes, rising into the air of new life. Just as the contents of the unconscious mind had teased and flirted with consciousness, now the dead-and-resurrected Self will tease and flirt with external reality, seeking to find better revelations in the solid creation and in the "dry mountain ground" of Mt. Ararat, the mountain of spiritual ascent.

Having completed the watery journey inward (the journey of self-understanding), the Self is now on solid ground, fulfilled by a successful harmony between consciousness and unconsciousness. The result is freedom from navel-gazing and a movement from passivity to activity in the "objective" world. The one who was tapped and taunted now does the tapping and taunting. After the journey inward come the freedom and the energy for the journey out. After the water come the fire, and the air, and the earth.

> —From *Views from the Intersection: Poems and Meditations,* by Virginia Ramey Mollenkott and Catherine Barry, p. 65

REFLECTIVE READING

Invite all to face North. Have earth symbols present for all to see. If the service is held outdoors, invite all to touch the earth, or drop soil to the earth as a reverent action of returning all creation, all life, to the earth. Then continue the reading "The North."

THE NORTH

When we think of North, we think of mystery and power. There is a mysteriousness about this direction because it is never reached by the Sun; it speaks of the unknown, the unseen. The North is a powerful direction too. Consider how the skies all revolve around the North Star. Because of its power and mystery, the North symbolizes the power to be silent and listen, to keep secrets; it represents the earth, midnight, winter, and black.

REFLECTIVE QUESTIONS

Have soft music playing in the background. Reflect on these questions:

- How is the phoenix, the fire bird, represented in my life?

- What images in the reading spark life or questions in me?

FAITH SHARING

Share your reflections on the questions and readings with each other.

CLOSING PRAYER

GUIDE ME INTO AN UNCLENCHED MOMENT

Gentle me, Holy One,
into an unclenched moment,
a deep breath,
a letting go
of heavy expectancies,
of shriveling anxieties,
of dead certainties,
that, softened by the silence,
surrounded by the light,
and open to the mystery,
I may be found by wholeness,
upheld by the unfathomable
entranced by the simple,
and filled with the joy
that is you.

—From *Guerrillas of Grace,*
by Ted Loder, p. 17

SIGN OF PEACE

In silence join hands in a circle and experience the love, support, and power of God in the silence. Join hands for three or four minutes.

Air (East)

PREPARATION AND SYMBOLS

Have pictures of clouds, blowing trees, sand, and people. Consider having the service outdoors; use wind chimes. Use meditative "wind sounds" from a record or cassette tape. Place these items on a table or altar facing the East.

CALL TO PRAYER

Presider: Provident God, come to our assistance.

All: God, make haste to help us.

Presider: Let justice travel like the wind.

All: And integrity like an unfailing breath.

Presider: Rise, O Breath of Life, raise your hand,
do not forget the poor.

All: You yourself have seen the distress and grief,
you watch and take them into your hands.

Presider: Holy One, you listen to the wants of the humble,
you bring strength to their hearts.

All: Breath of Life,
you grant them a hearing,
judging in favor of the orphaned and the exploited,

so that earthborn women and men
may strike fear no longer.

PSALMS 54 AND 69

A PSALM REFLECTION

*Benjamin F. Chavis, Jr., and nine other black activists were imprisoned
for their civil rights struggles in the 1970s. During his time in prison,
he reflected on his prison experiences in the form of psalms.*

Left: Blessed are the people who cry,
who moan and groan for relief
in the struggle for liberation.
For God, our ultimate liberator,
shall bring to pass an end to oppression;
our tears of sorrow shall become tears of joy.

Right: Blessed are those who suffer,
who are in pain and torture because of inhumanity,
for God our holy comforter shall terminate the agony —
our wounds shall be healed.

Left: Blessed are the people who mourn,
who lament and weep over the cruel state of existence,
for God, our sustaining redeemer,
shall deliver those who cry out for God's help;
through God our fate is assured.

Right: Blessed are those who are patient,
who struggle on relentlessly,
having complete faith in God,
for God our liberation and salvation
shall always be on time.

All: O God, my God and savior,
you are the breath of my soul,
the essence of my spirit.
I yearn for your love;
I long for your salvation.

O God, my God and creator,
you are the foundation of my existence,
the undergirding force of my life.
I yearn for your love;
I long for your liberation.

— Adapted from *Psalms from Prison,* by
Benjamin F. Chavis, Jr.

READING

A BREATH OF KETTELER'S SPIRIT

As people who believe in Providence, we echo German social reformer Bishop Ketteler's words of September 21, 1848.

... Oh, yes, I believe in the truth of all these sublime ideas that are stirring the world to its very depths today.... But there is only one means of realizing these sublime ideals — return to Him who brought them into the world, to the Son of God. Jesus Christ. Christ proclaimed those very doctrines.... He not only preached them — He practiced them and showed us the only way to make them part and parcel of our lives. He is the Way, the Truth, and the Life; outside of Him there is error, and lying, and death.... With Him, in the truth which He taught, on the Way which He pointed out, we can make a paradise on earth, we can wipe away the tears from the eyes of the poor, we can establish the reign of love, of harmony, and of fraternity — of true humanity! We can — I say it from the deepest conviction of my soul — we can establish community of goods and everlasting peace, and at the same time live under a free political institution. Without Him we shall perish disgracefully, miserably, the laughing-stock of succeeding generations. This is the solemn truth that speaks to us out of these graves: the history of the world bears it out. May we take it to heart!

— Bishop William Emmanuel Von Ketteler,
Founder of the Sisters of Divine Providence

RESPONSE

Glory be to God whose power in us
can do infinitely more than we can ask or imagine.

REFLECTIVE READING

Before the reader begins the reflection on the East, invite all to stand and face the East. Participants can listen to the sound of chimes or music of "wind sounds." Then continue with the reading.

THE EAST

Because the sun rises in the East, this direction is characterized by the dawn, by new beginnings, like the springtime, the breath of new life on the earth. The East's colors are pale ones like those of the dawn and the spring. As the South represents the "will" so the East corresponds to the mind, the ability to comprehend truth.

Take time apart to reflect, face East, and breathe deeply the life of God.

- How do I breathe forth elements needed to create nourishing community with (*a*) family and friends, and (*b*) our sisters and brothers of different traditions?

- Tell stories about nourishing groups you have been part of. How has the Breath of God moved the group?

FAITH SHARING

As you gather together to share, choose a song that is meaningful to the group. It may have elements of air, spirit, hope, etc., in which God is the Breath of Life. Share in faith your insights on the questions and readings. Play the music while regathering the group.

CLOSING PRAYER

Presider: God, our creator and sustainer,
you loved us long before we knew ourselves to be lovable
and love us still.
Give us, we pray,
a greater awareness of your love for all people,
and a confidence in the action of your grace
in us and in your church.

Inspire us with a greater sensitivity
to the poor and oppressed.
Give us the courage to act on their behalf.
We praise you today for your mysterious ways among us:
for your presence in the midst of human affairs
and your seeming absence.
By the power of your Spirit,
may we grow in the truth that impels us to act justly,
and thus give expression
to the compassion of your child, Jesus.
This we ask through this same Jesus Christ
who lives among us as friend and savior.
Amen.

SIGN OF PEACE

Water (West)

PREPARATION AND SYMBOLS

Have a glass or chalice of water or wine. Place a basin of water in the center of the circle.

CALL TO PRAYER

Presider: Earth Maker, come to our assistance.

All: God, make haste to help us.

Presider: Let justice flow like water.

All: And integrity like an unfailing stream.

Presider: Rise, gentle flowing God, raise your hand,
do not forget the poor.

All: You yourself have seen the distress and grief,
you watch and take them into your hands.

Presider: Gentle God, you listen to the want of the humble,
you bring strength to their hearts.

All: Grant them a hearing,
judging in favor of the orphaned and the exploited
so that earthborn women and men
may strike fear no longer.

PRAYER

Magnificat — Luke 1:47–55. Another version of the Magnificat can be found in Image-Breaking — Image-Building, *by Linda Clark, Marion Ronan, and Eleanor Walker, Pilgrim Press, p. 68.*

PRAYERS OF CELEBRATION AND CONCERN

Response: Grant this, O Creator Lord!

- We thank you God for your love that became flesh and lived among us in the person of Jesus Christ. May we follow your example in loving your people . . .

  Response and pause after each prayer.

- We thank you God for the great people of faith: Sarah, Deborah, Abraham, Moses, and Ruth. For Teresa of Avila, Catherine of Siena, and Ambrose. For Dorothy Day, Thomas Merton, Martin Luther King, Jr., Dorothy Kazel, Ita Ford, Maura Clarke, and Jean Donovan. May the shining example of these people of faith encourage and strengthen us in our journey . . .

- We thank you God for our sisters and brothers who labor with the poor and oppressed at home and abroad, especially those in Puerto Rico, El Salvador, Korea, Peru, and Nicaragua. Let us all remember and support them. Give them the courage and strength to bring justice and peace to our people . . .

- We thank you God for the wonderful work you are doing in our world today, liberating and freeing others to be fully what you have called them to be. Help us to be faithful to this inner truth that you have written in our hearts.

- We thank you for and ask your blessing on our sisters and brothers in ministry in all faith-traditions. May their work bear much fruit . . .

- We thank you God for all our fathers and mothers, grandmothers and grandfathers, aunts and uncles, sisters and brothers, and nieces and nephews. May they be faithful to your call for them. And may you grant eternal rest to those whom you have called home...

- We thank you God for our many friends in community and in our family with whom we study, live, and minister side by side. May the time we spend with them be a sacred time of sharing and caring...

PRAYER

RIVER WATER FOR SALE

The Master's sermon that day consisted of only one enigmatic sentence.

He just gave a wry smile and began, "All I do here is sit by the bank of the river, selling river water."

And with that he ended his sermon.

He had set up his stall on the river bank, the waterseller, and thousands came to buy water from him. The whole success of his trade depended on their not seeing the river. When they finally saw it, he ran out of business.

The preacher was a great success. Thousands came to learn wisdom from him. When they got the wisdom, they stopped coming to his sermons. And the preacher smiled contentedly. For he had attained his purpose, which was to bow out as quickly as possible for he knew in his heart that he was only offering people what they already had, if they would only open their eyes and see. "Unless I go," said Jesus to his disciples, "the Holy Spirit will not come."

•

If you stopped selling water so vigorously people might have a better chance of seeing the river.

— From *Song of the Bird,*
by Anthony de Mello, SJ, p. 74

REFLECTIVE READING

Invite all to turn toward the West and face the water symbols. If you are outside, face a lake or pond. Then begin the reading "The West."

THE WEST

The West, the direction in which the sun sets, symbolizes twilight and autumn. Its colors are the deeper shades of blues, purples, and greens, the colors of the twilight sky and the waters that become indistinguishable from it. The darkening skies and waters in the West are like the deeper feelings that emerge in the autumn or twilight of one's life.

REFLECTIVE QUESTIONS

Take time apart to reflect on the following questions:

Let stories surface within. Name how you are open to life flowing, moving, probing, growing...

- as woman or man
- in weakness
- in denying my strength
- by my fear of losing control if I love too much

GATHERING SONG

Play "Come to the Water," by John Foley, SJ. While the song, or instrumental music, is playing, invite each person to take the common cup, hold it, and look into the water. See beyond where you are in time and dare to see into the future. Quietly give thanks of God. When finished, give the cup to the next person.
Share thoughts from the reflection time.

CLOSING PRAYER

God of our hope,
we give thanks for this day and these people,
and for the gospel that gives this day meaning
and your people direction.

Stay close to us.
Do not pass from our view lest we lose our way and our heart.

Encourage us. Root us in you.
Make us so desire your life in us that our only fear is your absence
and our greatest joy is your love.

RITUAL BLESSING

Bless each other with water.

Creation

Have clay pots filled with different colors of soil. Use framed pictures of the earth placed around the room or on a table.

INTRODUCTION

Invite people to prayer with music. Have flute or soft piano music in the background with dimmed lights in the room. After a few minutes the reading follows.

READING

From ancient times, the earth has represented the feminine — seen as nourishing, rhythmic, fertile, and mysterious. We humans are wed to the earth . . . born from her, we return to her in death. Today as we pause for prayer, we celebrate earth . . . our physical selves and the senses that enable us to find our Creator God in the matter of our universe.

READING

Even plants and trees no longer have enough air to breathe, or enough water, or are simply removed. Entire forests, which serve as recreational areas for people who live in big cities, have been cut down and cleared, in order to create still more business for the airlines or even to accommodate military airplanes equipped with bombs. Slowly but surely we are ruining the earth we live on, without consideration for those who live on it after us. . . .

The Eskimos, the Hopi Indians, the original native Australians have an entirely different relationship with the earth. They say that the earth knows nothing about the words "mine" and "yours."

> *— Not Just Yes and Amen,* by Dorothee Soelle
> and Fulbert Steffensky, pp. 28–29

MUSIC AND RITUAL

Use Indian music (obtain a record from a library) or any soft music. At this time pass around the clay pots. Invite people to touch, trace symbols in the earth, be part of the earth. The leader begins the ritual. During this time, with soft music in the background, the "Canticle of All Creation," by Francis of Assisi, is read (by two readers):

Left: Most High, all powerful, all good Lord!
All praise is yours, all glory, all honor, and all blessing.
To you alone, Most High, do they belong.
No mortal lips are worthy to pronounce your name.

Right: All praise be yours, my Lord,
through all that you have made,
and first my Lord Brother Sun,
who brings the day,
and light you give us through him.
How beautiful is he, how radiant in all his splendor!
Of you, Most High,
he bears the likeness.

Left: All praise be yours, my Lord,
through Sister Moon and Stars,
in the heavens you have made them
bright and precious and fair.

Right: All praise be yours, my Lord,
through Brother Wind and Air,
and fair and stormy, all the weather's moods,
by which you cherish all that you have made.

Left:	All praise be yours, my Lord, through Sister Water, so useful, lowly, precious and pure.
Right:	All praise be yours, my Lord, through Brother Fire, through whom you brighten up the night. How beautiful he is, how gay. Full of power and strength.
Left:	All praise be yours, My Lord, through Sister Earth, our Mother, who feeds us in her sovereignty and produces various fruits with colored flowers and herbs.
Right:	All praise by yours, my Lord, through those who grant pardon for love of you; those who endure sickness and trial, happy those who endure in peace, by you, the Most High, they will be crowned.
Left:	All praise be yours, my Lord, through Sister Death, from whose embrace no mortal can escape. Woe to those who die in sin. Happy those she finds doing your will. The second death can do no harm to them.
All:	Praise and bless the Lord, and give thanks. And serve with great humility.

—St. Francis of Assisi

PRAYER

Share personal prayers of gratitude and thanks for creation and all good gifts.

FINAL BLESSING

Given by a leader who might extend hands out over the group and pray.

Anointing for Mission

PREPARATION

Have container(s) of oil or lotion. As an alternative to anointing one another on the forehead, it might be desirable to put lotion on the person's hands and gently massage them while offering silent prayer or greeting.

Be sure to work out a clear procedure for distributing lotion and anointing so that people do not feel ill at ease with the ritual.

CALL TO PRAYER

Leader: As a mother hen gathers her young around her

All: So too does the Spirit of God shelter us
in the shadow of her wings.

Leader: As a woman celebrates
when the lost coin has been found

All: So too does our God rejoice
when she finds compassion
in the hearts of her children.

Leader: As Mary recognized human need
at the wedding feast in Cana
and made it known to her child.

All: So is our God moved by the needs of her people
and makes them known to us.

PRAYER

All: We hear your call and are surprised
that you invite us again to share in your ministry.
Our zeal in the past has not set worlds on fire
and our attachment to convenience
shields us from the urgency of needs around us.
And yet you call,
and leave us wondering what you see in us.
Give up on us already. Be done with us!
We disappoint you and ourselves.
Have you no one else but us?

READING

*Taken from the charter, constitutions, or mission statement of the group
that gathers.*

SONG

*"Spirit of God," by Gregory Norbet, OSB, "Earthen Vessels," by John
Foley, SJ, or another song.*

READING: *Luke 4:14–21*

HOMILY

ANOINTING

Leader: Spirit of power,
time and again throughout history
you have anointed your servants and sent them on mission:
to speak your word to the poor,
to heal the sick,
to free captives —

always renewing the face of the earth
in such a variety of ways
that creation itself sings of your glory
and the human family reflects your beauty
in a thousand different ways!

Leader extends hands over the oil.

Leader: Come Spirit of the Living One.
Bless this oil of anointing.
Make it an oil of gladness and of healing,
a lotion of strength and tenderness.
We pray that by this anointing
our hands and hearts might be strengthened
for the work that lies ahead,
that we might be compassionate to human need,
tender and strong in our care for one another,
genuine in our friendship,
and faithful to the commitments we have made.

All: We pray
that through the power of this compelling Spirit,
we might know the unity that is ours:
sisters and brothers of a common family,
sharing a single home on this, our earth,
as children of one God.

With this shared hope and faith, we ask your blessing
as we anoint one another for the work of the gospel.

Leader begins the anointing.

GREETING OF PEACE

SONG

*"Anthem," by Tom Conry, "Our Life Is More Than Our Work," by
Charlie King, or another song.*

In Memory of...

Use roses or carnations or even wildflowers. As the service progresses decide what flowers will be used according to what is available and appropriate. The vases are to be empty on the table as the service begins. You will need three different kinds of flowers. One will represent the present, one the past, and another the future. Ask a variety of people to do the readings.

The presider welcomes the guests and gathers people for prayer.

INTRODUCTION

When we remember heroes of war, as our country does on days like Veterans' Day, we are also prone to remember heroes in our own lives.

Today we pray in memory of family members and friends who have been vibrant, spirit-filled people throughout history.

We pray for all — "in memory" of those who have made a difference in others' lives because they have had a life of living according to values and beliefs that were important to them.

Today we pray "in memory" of outstanding, yet gentle, loving people, people who throughout our early history were struck with poverty. Today there are so many of our brothers and sisters who suffer the same oppression.

We pray "in memory" of all here present, for our sharing a concern for the future, sharing knowledge, sharing faith, keeping informed, and doing our part. We pray "in memory" of each of you who continue to have concern for the oppressed, those in need of knowing the loving presence of God in our world, and for standing with others as prophetic people, helping to bring about a more just society.

PRAYER AND RITUAL FOR THE PAST

Five or six people are given flowers to hold while the following is read:

IN MEMORY OF OUR PAST!

To be read with passion:

So we look again at our foreparents and realize that this is living by faith and by love. People who live this way are seeking a homeland, go to a homeland, bring in and embrace a homeland. These crazy, wild sojourners desire a better country than the secure, legalistic land of security. They desire a better country, that is, a heavenly one. God has already prepared for them a city. What a wild company we belong to. I mean, do you understand? These are our foreparents. These are the founders of our faith. These are the old alumni. These are the ones who established, with their sweat and tears, the "institution." These wild people, persecuted people, going out, not-knowing-where-they're-going people. These are our foreparents we remember....

> — Adapted from "In the Company of the Faithful," by Vincent Harding, in *Sojourners,* May 1985

Those holding the flowers name a person and a memory about the individual while going forward to place their flowers in the one empty vase. There can be pictures of people already deceased placed around that vase. Others in the group can offer names also. As the responses subside the next reading is presented.

PRAYER AND RITUAL FOR THE PRESENT

Five or six others are given a different kind of flower to hold while the reading for the present takes place.

IN MEMORY OF OUR PRESENT!

To be read with conviction:

If this is our ancestral faith community, then what are *we* called to be? Has the work all been done? So now can we sit and relax, believing the dangerous part is finished? The texts from Scripture speak to our hearts, speaks to our lives, as if to say, "Listen sisters and brothers, we are surrounded by such a great crowd of witnesses." Do you know why these people surround us on all sides? Not so we can admire them and talk about them and wave banners before their pictures. All of that is okay, but not sufficient. They are here so they can fill us with courage and strength and life, in the great tradition of the wild baptizer by the Jordan, in the company of the lover on the cross. They are here to help us continue on in the struggle, the same struggle that they knew so well. Let us run the race, let us run with perseverance the race that is set before us, looking to Jesus, the pioneer and perfector of our faith. These are our present-day witnesses. . . .

> —Adapted from Heb. 12:1–2, by Vincent Harding, "In the Company of the Faithful, *Sojourners,* May 1985

Those holding the flowers name a present-day person and something about him or her and go forward and place their flowers in another vase. Surrounding that vase can be pictures of present-day prophetic people. Some might even be pictures of people in your group gathered for prayer.

PRAYER AND RITUAL FOR THE FUTURE

Another five or six people are given a third kind of flower to hold during this reading.

THINKING OF OUR FUTURE!

To be read with hope:

It is very clear that the way of our foreparents and our way is to get out of hiding places, to stand up, not to be afraid, to admit we're not sure of the next step, but to stand and know that we are not alone. We know we are surrounded by a company, by a gathering, by a whole bunch of folks who care for us, because we're part of the same wild community, citizens of a country, with faces and names unknown to us right now, that does not yet exist — and yet *does*. For our future members who will join our company....

— From "In the Company of the Faithful,"
by Vincent Harding, in *Sojourners,* May 1985

At this time the flower-bearers take the flowers to another vase and name future people. Pictures of babies can be placed around the vase.

SONG

"We Are a Gentle, Loving People," by Holly Near. You might design your own verses. Use a song that most people present know. If someone knows how to play a musical instrument, a song played by that person would be very appropriate.

CLOSING READING

Jesus the Word was the pioneer of our faith both before and after Jesus of Nazareth. It was this compelling Word who drew all those long-ago people out of their safe places, out of their quiet places, out of their easy places and said, *There is a city that needs to be created,* and I want you to put your hands, your hearts, your minds to work.

These all died in faith, not having received what was promised, but having seen it and greeted it from afar, and having acknowledged that they were strangers and exiles on the earth. For people who speak thus make it clear that they are seeking a homeland. If they had been thinking of that land from which they had gone out, they would have had opportunity to return.

But as it was, they desired a better country, that is, a heavenly one. Therefore God is not ashamed to be called their God, for God has prepared for them a city...

Therefore, since we are surrounded by so great a cloud of witnesses, let us also lay aside every weight and sin that clings so closely, and let us run with perseverance the race that is set before us, looking to Jesus the pioneer and perfector of our faith, who for the joy that was set before

him endured the cross, despising the shame, and is seated at the right
hand of the throne of God.

—Hebrews 10:32–35; 11:1–2, 5–16, 35–40;
12:1–2; from "In the Company of the
Faithful," by Vincent Harding, in *Sojourners,*
May 1985

CONCLUSION

*Soft music might be played in the background as the leader invites all to
join together and continue the celebration over foods brought by guests.*

Strength of Women

Leader: Praise the One who has heard the cry of the poor,

All: Who has lifted up the weak
and given them strength.

Leader: Praise the One who has fed the hungry
and satisfied the longing of those in need,

All: Who has held with tenderness the orphan and widow
and given the stranger a land and home.

ANTIPHONAL PRAYER

Left: My spirit takes delight in the presence of our God;
my heart is filled with laughter
and my words fall short of the truth I long to express.

Right: For the One whom I love is faithful:
our ancestors have known compassion throughout the ages,
and this day, mercy is given us.

Left: Holy is the love
and sacred is the place where we meet.
We are in awe of the gift that is ours.

Right: The powerful have stumbled
and the rich are burdened and fall.
The proud are alone in their confusion.

Left: While before our eyes, the weak are upheld in kindness.
The poor are called by name; ·
the hungry are nourished with bread that never grows old.

Right: The promise endures.
The One whom we love is faithful
and life gives birth to beauty and truth.

All: Our Spirits take delight
in the wondrous presence of our God.
Holy is this love.
We are in awe of the gift that is ours.

—Based on Luke 2:46–55

SONG

"El Shaddai," by Colleen Fulmer, or "Wherever You Go," by Gregory Norbet, OSB. In the songbook that accompanies Cry of Ramah *by Colleen Fulmer, Martha Ann Kirk, CCVI, offers simple gestures to accompany "El Shaddai." Please see the Resources section, p. 179.*

Refrain:

El Shaddai, Mother who shelters, under your wings,
in the sweetness of life or bitter pain.

1. Do not ask me to leave you,
   I will stay by your side,
   tender God who cares for the orphan
   who is so longing to provide.

2. I will go where you journey
   and our lives will entwine
   your own people as my people
   and your God will be mine.

3. Old woman, younger daughter,
   precious widow, orphan child,
   Mother God who knows all your longings,
   who from the struggle births a child.

— "El Shaddai," by Colleen Fulmer

READING

The book of Ruth is a story of human liberation. In a male-dominated society Naomi and Ruth must determine their own survival without the benefit of husbands. The two widows initiate the actions. Even when Boaz intervenes, he is responding to their initiatives. In a man's world these two women are center stage. They are the catalysts for divine intervention. They shock, they provoke, they intimidate. Ruth is the story of two women responding to the limitations of a patriarchal society. Naomi and Ruth demonstrate the delicate art of coping and caring in a remarkably feminine way. Theirs is the story of human persons who yearn to contribute to the community in the face of all obstacles.

Today we are asked to look at our lives, personally and corporately, and to renew life, to nurture life, to share life in ways we have not done before. We are called to root ourselves more deeply in God, to reach within ourselves to take new risks and perhaps, as in Ruth, to give up our homeland — the way things have been, the way we have always done things. We are called to love who we are in God so much that we have no alternative. In doing this we will discover a new future, a new life, because we have become fertile again.

— Rita Petruziello, CSJ

OPPORTUNITY FOR SHARING AND PRAYER

PRAYER

All: Loving God, we celebrate your faithfulness and love,
         and praise you for the wonders you have worked
         through women and men of faith throughout history.

         Your presence within us enables us
         to claim our own strength and our need,

and to take risks in the service of your people,
confident of your grace.

Continue to root us more deeply in your love
that any life that results from our efforts
might be an expression of your truth and love.
We ask this through your child, Jesus,
your own word and gift of love. Amen.

SONG

"Something About the Women," by Holly Near, or another song of celebration of gifts.

Refashion a People

PREPARATION

Have an earthenware or glass container of soil, an earthenware or glass pitcher of water, and a short tree branch.

OPENING PRAYER

All: God of all life,
we give you thanks for the signs
of your love that surround us;
for sun and warmth
and all that comes to life within creation;
for all that sleeps within the earth
awaiting birth.
We praise you for the wisdom
of your touch:
water on the earth,
sunlight on spirits,
hands on blinded eyes.
Continue to touch us.
Reach out to us
with compassion and forgiveness,
that knowing ourselves to be loved and graced,
we might work to bring about your Reign.
Amen.

SONG

"Mantle of Light," by Colleen Fulmer, or other song that recalls creation or baptism.

RITUAL

During the song, the leader pours water on the earth and stirs it with the tree branch. It may be necessary to pour water a second time, stirring again until the soil has the consistency of mud.

1. Mantle of Light, Risen Christ,
   Spirit enfolding,
   healing and holding
   all that I was, all that I am,
   all that I'll ever hope to be.

2. Gentlest rain, touching with kindness,
   calming, restoring, cleansing, transforming
   the child that I was, child that I am,
   child that I'll ever hope to be.

3. O God, Loving God, let me rest in your care,
   like a child in the arms of her mother,
   knowing such tenderness there....

4. Wind blowing free, Breath of Creation,
   forming in me,
   love that will speak to the world that we were,
   world that we are,
   world that we'll ever hope to be.

— "Mantle of Light," by Colleen Fulmer

ANTIPHONAL PRAYER

Left: We praise you, God, for sparkling water,
          for life-soaked earth
          replete with promise.

Right: Pour over us this water of rebirth.
Hover over us, as first your Spirit lingered
when we were but a hope of yours.

Left: Take up again this clay.
Refashion and reform
until your image once more is mirrored.
We ask you to take care,
for clay is fragile and
earthenware breaks easily.

Right: Hold all within your hands:
our past and future, our ever-present birth.
Our eyes are caked with mud
not yet washed away.
Our ears and tongues still silenced.

Left: Inscribe the ground again.
Write names and deeds we'll gladly claim
to be so noticed and so known by you.

Right: Use all the waters of creation;
birth us, wash us clean.
Use all the earth your hands have made
and give us home and shelter
in our hearts of flesh.

All: Awake us now.
Unbind us; call us forth.
We know ourselves alive.

The leader invites those gathered to recall and mention passages from Scripture in which mud, clay, or water is mentioned.

QUESTIONS FOR REFLECTION

- How have we shaped each other?

- How have we been fashioned by each other,
  felt each others' hands in our lives?

- What rough edges have been smoothed?

or

- What has come together or been shaped by our common enterprise?

- What are the events of our lives and of these days that are shaping us?

- How are we being fashioned by these events?

or

- Continued reflection on any of the Scripture passages shared previously

OPPORTUNITY FOR SHARING AND PRAYER

RITUAL

When the time given to reflection is completed, the leader invites those gathered to inscribe their initials, a symbol of themselves, in the mud; or the leader might draw some symbol that is expressive of the group as a whole. Instrumental music or the song used earlier might be played.

READING

Rise up, child of earth,
let life rise up in you,
full-term, new born.
Time enough in wondrous darkness,
echoed sounds of voices, stirrings,
splashings of new life.
Relinquish to memory this one mystery
we yearn to know and will again
in after-death.
So much latent
still to rise
until our rising lifts us to a depth
that questions every truth
we've ever known.

Mud-stirred of first-clay.
Plaything of a potter who fell in love
with her hands' work.
Blessed be her handiwork.
Blessed be the work of her hands.
Blessed be.

Mud stirred of first sight
of one long since born blind.
So grand an opening to see at last
this mid-life child of multi-colored song
and brilliant dance.
Blessed be.

So much latent
still to see, to dance, to sing
until our rising lifts us to the depths
of that first spring of living water
that spilled us forth in mud and birth
So long ago and still today.
Blessed we.
Blessed be.

—Pat Kozak, CSJ

BLESSING

Leader: May the gentleness of spring rains
           soften the tensions within us,
           and the power of ocean waves
           steady and strengthen us.
           May the wisdom of the earth
           open us to mystery.
           Let the music of its forest streams
           delight us
           and the simplicity of its wildflowers
           captivate our hearts.

All: May our ever-creating God continue to bless us.
           Amen. Blessed be God.

Letting Go Through Death

PREPARATION

Have a table that can be seen by all. Place an earthen bowl containing water on the table. Have incense ready.

SONG

"We Remember, We Celebrate, We Believe," by Marty Haugen, or a favorite song of the deceased person.

READING

William W. Warren was born in May 1825, the son of an Ojibway mother and a white father. His ancestry revealed that he was a descendant of Richard Warren, one of the "Mayflower" pilgrims. As a child he was educated in mission schools and eastern institutions. Warren died at the age of twenty-eight, just having completed the first of three projected works on the history of his nation, based on the Ojibway traditions and oral statements. The following passage describes his people.

When an Ojibway dies, the body is placed in a grave, generally in a sitting posture, facing the West. With the body are buried all the articles needed in life for a journey. If a man, his gun, blanket, kettle, fire steel, flint, and moccasins; if a woman, her moccasins, axe, portage collar, blanket, and kettle. The souls are supposed to stand immediately after the death of the bodies, on a deep beaten path, which leads westward;

the first object they come to, in following this path, is the great Oda-e-min (Heart berry), or strawberry, which stands on the roadside like a huge rock, and from which they take a handful and eat on their way. They travel on till they reach a deep, rapid stream of water, over which lies the much dreaded Ko-go-gaup-o-gun, or rolling and sinking bridge; once safely over this as the travellers look back, it assumes the shape of a huge serpent swimming, twisting, and untwisting its folds across the stream. After camping out four nights, and travelling each day through a prairie country, the souls arrive in the land of the spirits, where they find their relatives accumulated since humankind was first created; all is rejoicing, singing, and dancing; they live in a beautiful country interspersed with clear lakes and streams, forests and prairies, and abounding in fruit and game to repletion — in a word, abounding in all that the red people most covets in this life, and which conduces most to their happiness. It is that kind of a paradise that they only by their manner of life on this earth are fitted to enjoy.

— Adapted from *History of the Ojibway People,*
by William W. Warren, pp. 72–73

RITUAL OFFERING

Have individuals bring in articles of the deceased that were important to her or him. Hold them up one at a time; tell a story about the object and its relationship to the friend. When this is completed place the article on a table. Invite others to share other stories. Then, incense the objects, praying that we who are present might continue in the spirit of this person.

Bless a bowl of strawberries. Pass them around for all to share and enjoy their rich, juicy flavor. During this ritual the leader prays:

Loving God, we thank you for ＿＿＿＿＿, who was so dear and beloved to us. We thank you that through her/his life and suffering, she/he became a person we all could love. We pray that all that ＿＿＿＿＿ held dear will be remembered and honored by those who come after her/him. We ask that her/his special gifts will continue to be valued by us long after her/his death. We pray that nothing of ＿＿＿＿＿'s life will be lost, but that her/his spirit will remain in our hearts and give strength to us in our times of need. We thank you, God, that the life-giving spirit and presence of _____ will go on living in our hearts, in our minds, in our lives, and in this holy ground, Mother Earth.

MUSIC

Soft music can be played in the background, possibly "Four Seasons" by Vivaldi. A leader comes forward, takes the vessel of water, and sprinkles those gathered with water as she or he prays:

I sprinkle you with water, this sacred sign of life, asking that you be embraced by Mother Earth as we are fed with the warm memories of our friend, _____ .

Enable us to continue the journey with pride and joy in our remembrance of the life of this holy person. May we have courage and strength to live a life filled with this penetrating Spirit of God.

Blessed are you, Creator and Sustainer of life. May your holy care be upon these people who are blessed in your name and who are sustained in your love. Amen.

Join in sharing festive foods. More strawberries can be served.

Church

Leader: Your Word, O God, is power and truth.

All: We have seen it with our own eyes and stand in awe.

Leader: You have chosen the weak to lift up the strong.

All: And have called the foolish to confound the wise.

Leader: We have seen your glory made manifest in the little ones of the earth,

All: And radiant in the eyes of the poor.

SONG

BLESSED IS SHE

Blessed is she, who believed
that the promise made her by our God
would be fulfilled, would be fulfilled.

1. And Mary said:
   "Let me sing the praise of God
   for having touched this lowly one
   and from now on I shall be called:
   'Woman most highly blessed.'

2. Holy is our God!
   whose kindness never ends
   who by great strength
   has scattered the proud
   and raises up the poor
   and gathers them into all fullness.

3. For God has come
   to this servant Israel
   to show all mercy
   now and forever
   as was promised Sarah and Abraham
   and their children forever."

— "Blessed Is She," by Colleen Fulmer

In the songbook that accompanies Cry of Ramah *by Coleen Fulmer, Martha Ann Kirk, CCVI, describes simple gestures that further enhance the song. Refer to the Resources section, p. 179.*
In the final refrain, it is possible to sing:

Blessed are we who believe
that the promise made us by our God
would be fulfilled, would be fulfilled.

PRAYER

All: You have called us to be church
          and we strive to be that faithfully.
          Yet still we find ourselves
          recalling only words and forgetting your Spirit.
          We remember law and often disregard life.
          We too often preside over mercy and dispense service,
          causing your church to become a place and not a people.
          Forgive us. Show us mercy.
          Let us see the truth as seen by you.
          Help us turn things right side up again,
          beginning with our hearts.

ANTIPHONAL PRAYER

Left: Strength did not turn your heart
nor did wisdom merit your attention.
"Small" was chosen. "Weak" was given glory.

Right: We have tried to change your way with us,
and have won position, honor, and prestige.
From those mistaken heights
we sought to pray and serve you.

Left: We yearned for you — with half our hearts,
but prayers were lost and voices muted.
And all we heard was our own echo
ringing out in isolation.

Right: While all the while, your eyes turned toward the poor,
your hands stretched out to those who hunger,
your heart enfolded those who mourn.
You stayed and waited in the midst of loving
until our yearning drew us back.

Left: If we would be church,
then we are poor and blind and hungry.
If we are church,
then we are justice, bread, and sight.

All: We pray for church to happen,
for courage and for truth.
We pray, in need, with all our hearts,
for church to be,
for us to be your church.

READING

A GENTLE PRESENCE

For the church to call itself to work as Jesus did, in poverty and under oppression, is to seek an unaccustomed stance. It is to be, stand, and operate from the point of view of the world's victims and losers. It is to live and to preach the gospel from the bottom up. It is a falling down, a downward mobility, if you will, into the commonality of human existence. It is neither nice nor comfortable. In addition, it is confrontational and conflictual.

Because of such a stance, the church, while it is committed to and in the world, will also be at odds with the world "as it is." Such obedience to God will necessarily mean it will be a minority phenomenon, a threat to any political or cultural status quo. The ramifications are many, the cost is high.

— Chuck Lathrop

OPPORTUNITY FOR SHARING AND PRAYER

PRAYER

All: We give you thanks for all
that you have worked within your church,
for all the service rendered and people loved.
We ask for strength and courage
that we might stand for truth
when all the systems that surround us
would urge us to abandon it or compromise.
Remind us of the roots from which we come:
a people small and weak,
of no account but that you love them,
and made of them a people and a church,
gave to them sisters and brothers,
and a future full of hope.

SONG

Any song of commitment or service.

Prayer

Have incense burning in the room. It can be lit as people enter. Give them each an unlit candle as they enter the room.

INVITATION

Invite individuals as they enter the room to take a place, facing different directions, in comfortable positions. Have a designated area where the prayer will take place.

READING

Ohiyesa, the Santee Dakota physician and author, spoke in 1911 about the manner in which his people worship:

In the life of the Indians there was only one inevitable duty — of prayer — the daily recognition of the Unseen and Eternal. Their daily devotions were more necessary to them than daily food. They wake at daybreak, put on their moccasins and step down to the water's edge. Here they throw handfuls of clear, cold water into their face, or plunge in bodily. After the bath, they stand erect before the advancing dawn, facing the sun as it dances upon the horizon, and offer their unspoken orison. Their mates may precede or follow them in their devotions, but never accompany them. Each soul must meet the morning sun, the new sweet earth, and the Great Silence alone!

Whenever, in the course of the daily hunt the red hunters come upon a scene that is strikingly beautiful or sublime — a black thundercloud with the rainbow's glowing arch above the mountain, a white waterfall in the heart of a green gorge, a vast prairie tinged with the blood-red of sunset — they pause for an instant in the attitude of worship. They see no need for setting apart one day in seven as a holy day, since to them all days are God's.

— Adapted from *The Soul of the Indian,* by
Charles A. Eastman, p. 36

GUIDED REFLECTION

Believing in the Indian tradition of taking time to pray as the moment calls for, let us pause now and in our memories recall moments, people, or events that are special to us.

The leader invites all to relax, close their eyes, and rest where they are. Begin reading the following meditation.

Face a direction that you like. Directly in front of you is a road. Follow it and pause at places along the path. Listen.... Notice what is around you.... The path will lead you to a stream. The stream has water rippling in circular motions. Watch the circling waters go deeper and deeper. Explore these waters. If you have any particular memory you want to experience, take time now to allow that memory to come alive before you.

Take a deep breath. Continue to breathe in and breathe out. Enter into your memories. Take time to search,... to explore,... to look at your memories. Name those you want to experience and spend time being with them now.

Allow five to ten minutes.

Take time now to return. Breathe in and out, slowly, being aware of your breathing. Breathe in and out. As you exhale now come back to the road and leave the stream. Follow the path back to its beginning. Stand there quietly and own your Source of Power and Life.

RITUAL

As the above reflection ends, put soft music on or have someone sound a drum with a slow, constant beat. Allow the song or sound to continue for a few moments.

Depending on the size of the group, one or two persons could light the candles each is holding and go to others to light their candles while saying to each: "I give light to the memories you hold dear to you. Arise and bring them and yourself to our circle." Each person comes forward with lighted candles, to a designated circle joining the other participants.

Have lights off or dimmed in the room. The only light will be the candles in the circle. Invite all to share their memories. The leader could begin.

After those who would like have had the opportunity to talk about their memories, all the candles can be put in the center of the circle, making one large light. The leader then incenses all the candles and someone prays aloud:

We want you, O Spirit of Truth,
to hear our gratitude that runs so deep:
For your great beauty,
for the deep lasting memories we can see and love seeing,
for noble light as it lavishes insights
and warmth and movement;
for the past we can feast, full of compassion and mercy,
for feeling and sustaining the desperate,
and for leading them visibly to conquer land of their own;
for the shape of truth, for holiness, for faithful love,
for the price paid, such is our God, a holy name!
And such are we.
We owe God our deepest truth, our holy response.
In wisdom we are one with our God.
Alleluia!

Weaver God

All: Weaver God, we come to you,
or — more the truth — you find us,
disconnected and out of sorts.
We are disheartened by our failures,
discouraged by our weakness,
and little that we do seems worthy of your grace.
Restore our fortunes. Restore our future.
Weave for us the tapestry
on which our lives are stretched.
Give us patience
with the endless back and forth
of shuttle, hand, and effort.
We look too closely,
seeing only strands and knots
and snarled threads of too-much-trying
or none-at-all.
Grant us eyes to see the whole
of which we are a part.
In the end, we ask for gentleness with ourselves,
acceptance of our less than perfect ways.
We pray that what we do and what you weave
form patterns clear to all,
of mercy in the warp of it
and love throughout.

SONG

"Yahweh," by Gregory Norbet, OSB, or another song.

ANTIPHONAL READING

LIFE LOOM

Reader 1:   Life loom,
we your thread
approach you with reverence, awe,
and infinite respect.

Reader 2:   Accept, please do —
the offering of ourselves,
our separate strands,
to be woven in and out, over, under, and through.
as we seek to become a part of you.

Reader 1:   You invite us to join you,
to add to and draw from,
the fabric of the world —
make us worthy of that invitation.

Reader 2:   Powerless we are, alone,
like clay without the potter's loving hands
or dough without the baker's kneading hands
we seek for communion, for fulfillment.

Reader 1:   How difficult it is to contribute to,
and not to control —
to utter that simple yes —
when really we would rather say not yet,
later, perhaps and perchance.

Reader 2:   Father Abraham, Mother Sarah too,
were invited to cast their fate to your loom —
worn out threads, frayed and tired,
and the weaver just pointed to the stars.

Reader 1:   What a tapestry you weave,
calling us beyond
our alone-ness and security,
definitions and boundaries,
to be surprised by miracles
of the textures now and to come —
Oh, if we could but perceive.

Reader 2:   Come follow me, you say,
and be shuttled back and forth, back and forth —
trust me, you say, trust me;
as the tapestry of days becomes the tapestry of weeks,
of months, and years of lives —

Reader 1:   What things you ask, what trust,
too much we say — Why?
Must we, like the grain of wheat, also die?
Why the gethsemanes, the golgothas?

Reader 2:   But the visions of tapestries remain
the patterns and fabric that could be,
that could be,
and life loom waits,
and calls through myriads of faces
in the collage of different tongues;
How can we escape you?
We cannot.

Reader 1:   Yes, though, is all you ask,
and indeed you ask all.
You know our failings and faults,
our frayed-ness and frailty,
and yet you call,
call our magnificent imperfections to fullness,

Reader 2:   Die and rise, you say,
die and rise;
and you fill our lives with crosses,
and empty graves,

as we are shuttled back and forth,
back and forth.

Reader 1: Out of our pain you weave joy,
out of our good Fridays, you weave Easters;
out of strands you weave a fabric, a tapestry.
Out of parts you weave a whole.

— Chuck Lathrop, in *A Gentle Presence*

OPPORTUNITY FOR SHARING AND PRAYER

PRAYER

All: We ask your blessing, Weaver God;
we need your steadfast presence.
In our discouragement and fatigue,
grant us laughter and support.
In our vision, give us zeal.
In our weakness, we ask that you accept us.
And in the beauty that is ours,
grant that we might stand in truth.
Bless us now, in all things good and human.
For all things woven and still to be,
we pray in thanks. Amen.

Mother of Exiles

PREPARATION

Have a collection of newspaper clippings about current events, national and local. Only the first paragraph or two of each is needed. Include the city and dateline in the reading.

READING

Prayer begins with someone reading the clippings, one after the other. After three or four have been read, a second reader begins speaking loudly enough to be heard above the first reader who continues with the current events. (It is helpful if the first reader lowers his or her voice a little.) The second person reads either Luke 10:25–37, the Good Samaritan, or Matthew 25:31–40, the Last Judgment. The current events reader stops suddenly, just as the scripture reader is beginning the last verse of the passage, so that the final line of the passage is heard by itself.

SONG

Select any song that is a prayer for mercy or strength.

PRAYER

All: Compassionate one,
         we are surrounded by the needs of your people

and are overwhelmed by their suffering.
We confess that so often the harm that comes to them
could be alleviated by our willingness
to share in their hardship,
by our efforts to end the injustice
that our systems and lifestyles help to support.

Have mercy on us, we pray.
Touch our hearts.
Open our eyes anew
that we might recognize our brothers and sisters
and be glad for the richness they bring to our family.
This we ask through Jesus, our brother and friend.

ANTIPHONAL PRAYER

Left: The days are coming, says our God,
when I will gather you.
The days are soon coming
when I will bring you to a land that I will show you,
a land of peace where justice reigns.

Right: The days are coming when I will cleanse you
of all that holds you in fear and terror,
of all that blinds you to truth.

Left: On that day, you will cry with those who mourn;
you will laugh with those rejoicing.
You will stand speechless before a newborn child,
and sing in joy before a mountain stream,
and all creation will give glory.

Right: The days are soon coming.
They are already here,
when I will give you a new heart
and you will know me.
On that day, the grain you have stored will feed the hungry.
The wealth you have saved will protect the poor,
and all children will find safe haven.

All: On that day,
all people will come into the land that God will show them,
a land of peace, where justice reigns
and all God's children will find safe haven.

READING: *Deuteronomy 10:12–22*

SONG

"God, Mother of Exiles," by Colleen Fulmer. In the songbook that accompanies Cry of Ramah *by Colleen Fulmer, Martha Ann Kirk, CCVI, offers a simple, yet powerful dance movement to accompany this song. Refer to the Resources section,* p. 179.

OPPORTUNITY FOR SHARING AND PRAYER

PRAYER

All: Mother of Exiles, Shelter of the Homeless,
we are in need of your mercy.
We ask your blessing on your children everywhere
who are in danger today.
Bless all who suffer from injustice.
Shelter them in the warmth of your love
and safeguard them from the evil that rages around them.
Turn our eyes and hearts to their needs
and give us courage to act for their good.
We ask this, relying on your compassion
and confident of your love. Amen.

Encircled by Creation

Place a carafe of water, a pot of earth, wind chimes, and a lit candle or burning incense in four different locations in the room, one element in each of the locations. If possible, situate these items along the outer ring of the seating area. Ask four different people to carry the elements at the appropriate time during the prayer.

Leader: We pray today, hoping to become more aware of the wholeness and holiness that are ours by our very identity as human persons, by virtue of our creation at the hand of a loving God, and by the power of the dream that lives within us.

    We celebrate this unity with our past and our future, within ourselves and with each other, with the larger communities of which we are a part, with our church and with our world.

    We believe with Teilhard de Chardin that because of creation, and still more powerfully because of the Incarnation, nothing is profane, nothing is unholy for those who know how to see. Everything is charged by the presence of God.

    We invoke the Spirit and her life-giving presence inherent in creation, to inspire and sustain our reflection and sharing today, to weave connections among us, linking us to each other, strengthening us from within and without.

We are invited to relax for a few minutes and allow the ancient elements of creation, the earth, air, water and fire, to encircle us, to ring round us, gracing us with their wisdom and joining us to each other.

Begin instrumental music, possibly that of the Japanese composer Kitaro or the music of Daniel Kobialka.

FIRE

Leader: We celebrate the gift of fire.

A person picks up lit candle or burning incense and circles the group during the reading. He or she then returns it to its stand.

Leader: We recognize the sun, creation's source of energy and life, and are in awe of its power to warm the death of winter into spring's green life. We close our eyes before its brilliance and still can feel its warmth and see its light against the shadow. Its radiance speaks of the divine power that has brought us into being, that today sustains and enlightens our life.

Let the sun's rays bathe each of us, the fire's heat warm us. Let its radiance penetrate deep within our spirit. Fire has held mystery since the beginning of time: Let there be light! Fire has purified and made sacred. It has symbolized immortality and the very Spirit of God. Fire communicates the presence of God and a passionate love of life and people. "Were not our hearts burning within us?" May the power, the warmth, the passion, and mystery of fire be given us.

AIR

Leader: We celebrate the gift of air.

A person takes wind chimes and carries them around the group during the reading. He or she then returns them to their stand.

Leader: Air is invisible and all pervasive, the force with which our Creator God breathed life into us. Without air we die.

It sustains every living plant and creature, and sculpts even rock into strange and beautiful shapes. Air is the breath of life.

We breathe deeply, and know our breathing to be a prayer, a communion with the source of life. The air that we breathe today is the same air breathed by great women and men who have gone before us, our ancestors and friends. The air that now fills our lungs was breathed by Sojourner Truth and Gandhi, by Oscar Romero and Martin Luther King, Jr., by Maura Clark and [name of person of significance to group], and by Jesus himself.

Great Spirit, whose voice we hear in the winds, whose power we feel in the raging storm, let your breath give life to our world.

WATER

Leader: The Spirit of Yahweh hovered over the water.
It is the gift of water we celebrate today.

A person picks up the carafe of water, circles the group during the reading, and then replaces the carafe on the stand.

Leader: No element is mentioned more often in Scripture: water for cleansing, water for baptism, for refreshment and life, water for transition from one stage of life to another, water for blessing.

We claim the water of life, whose rush announces the birth of a baby, a water of life that nourishes seeds and plant roots deep in the earth. We celebrate water without which all that lives would shrivel and wither away, water of our life.

"Come to me and I will give you living water, and you will never be thirsty again." Today we pray that our thirst be kept alive, until the justice that we thirst for is realized.

Today we celebrate our common thirst and the God who gifts us with water.

EARTH

Leader: We claim the gift of the earth.

A person takes the pot of earth, circles the group during the reading, and then replaces the earth on the stand.

Leader: From ancient times, the earth has been portrayed as feminine. Humankind has experienced the earth as lifegiving and nourishing, rhythmic and fertile.

We are radically joined with the earth, a mothering earth from whose womb all life comes, and to whose breast all life returns. It is by the fruits of this earth we live. On her lands we walk and play and love.

We pray that we might walk gently on this earth, that we might read her wisdom in every leaf and rock and field, and care for her with tender respect. Today we celebrate the earth, our own physical selves and all that enables us to find our Creator in the rich and varied gift of the universe.

As the reading is finished and people have been encircled and blessed by the individual elements, play the song "Breaths," by Sweet Honey in the Rock, "Canticle of the Sun," by Marty Haugen, or another song that captures the mystery and joy of creation. During this song, the symbols of earth, air, fire, and water are again carried around the room. Have persons who carry the elements encircle the room at the same time, walking in different directions so that the elements criss-cross each other, that people might experience themselves surrounded and enfolded by the grace of creation. When the song is nearly completed, persons gradually replace the elements on their stands and the prayer ends quietly.

Roundtable Ministry

PREPARATION

Have a round table in the center of the room, visible to all, perhaps with a bread plate and cup on the table. If no round table is available, hang a picture of a large circle or form a circle with rope or yarn on the floor. If numbers and space permit, arrange chairs in a circle.

CALL TO PRAYER

Leader: On the night before he died, Jesus, knowing what lay in store for him, drew his disciples to his side.

All: He had loved them throughout the years and now loved them in ways that words alone could not convey.

Leader: Jesus took up a basin of water and a towel and began to wash their feet.

All: And the disciples recognized Jesus in the act of service.

PRAYER

All: Once more our eyes are opened,
and we see you in our midst.
Yet still we hesitate;
still we fear to allow your truth to penetrate our hearts.

We are surprised.
We had not expected you to come this way.
We had not imagined you would act this way.
Stand still, we pray.
Your changes are too much for us!
We fear the cost of following you
and fear our loss if we do not.

SONG

"Lord Jesus," by Gregory Norbet, OSB, or another song of service.

READING

IN SEARCH OF A ROUNDTABLE

Concerning the why and how and what and who of ministry,
one image keeps surfacing:

A table that is round.

It will take some sawing
to be roundtabled,
some redefining
and redesigning.

Such redoing and rebirthing
of narrowlong churching
can painful be
for people and tables.

But so was the cross,
a painful too table
of giving and yes.

And from such death comes life,
from such dying comes rising,
in search of roundtabling.

And what would roundtable churching mean?

It would mean no diasing
and throning,
for but one king is there,
and he was a footwasher,
at table no less.

A healer of hearts, he,
and bestower of disturbing peace,
whose footsteps we lost track of.

We looked for signs,
but with uncircumcised hearts,
trying to discern
a message indiscernible
to pomped and circumstanced,
yet well intentioned ones,
who while proclaiming the finding,
were all the time losing.

For at the narrowlong tables,
servant and mirror
became picture framed
and centers of attention.

And crosses became
but gilded ornaments
on bare stone walls
in buildings used but once a week only.

But the times and the tables
are changing and rearranging.

And what of narrowlong table ministers,
when they confront
a roundtable people,
after years of working up the table
(as in "up the ladder")
to finally sit at its head,
only to discover
that the table has turned round?

Continued rarefied air
will only isolate
for there are no people there,
only roles.

They must be loved into roundness,
where *apart* is spelled *a part*
and the call
is to the gathering.

For God has called a People,
not "them and us."
"Them and us"
are unable
to gather round,
for at a roundtable,
there are no sides.

And *all* are invited
to wholeness and to food.

"When more than was lost
has been found has been found"
(e. e. cummings).

But wishing and hoping
will not get us there —
daily dying and rising will
(and some sawing).

At one time
our narrowlong churches
were built so to resemble the cross,
but it does no good
for buildings to do so,
if lives do not.

Roundtabling means
no preferred seating,
no first and last,
no better, and no corners
for "the least of these."

Roundtabling means
being with,
a part of,
together, and one.

It means room for the Spirit
and gifts
and disturbing profound peace for all.

It is no magic bread
that we are baking,
for the dough we are dealing with
must and will
take its dying-in-order-to-rise-again-time.

And it is we in the present
who are mixing and kneading
the dough for the future.

We can no longer prepare for the past.

We will and must and are called
to be Church,
and if He calls for other than roundtables
we are bound to follow.

Leaving behind the sawdust
and chips, designs and redesigns
behind.

All the while
being harmless as doves
and wily as serpents
in search of and in the presence of
the Kingdom
that is God's and not ours.

Amen.

—Chuck Lathrop, in *A Gentle Presence*

BRIEF QUIET

OPPORTUNITY FOR SHARING AND PRAYER

BLESSING

Leader: In the name of the One who came as servant,

All: We ask for compassion.

Leader: In the name of the poor from whom we must learn,

All: We ask for humility.

Leader: In the name of the oppressed
who have suffered too long,

All: We ask for a sense of urgency.

Leader: In the name of the Spirit who calls us,

All: We ask for integrity

Leader: Finally, in our own name
and in our need we pray.

All: Grant us the grace of your presence
and bless us with all that we need to serve you in truth.
Amen.

SONG

"Simple Gifts" (traditional Shaker hymn).

Transitions

PREPARATION

A ball of cord, possibly macramé, is needed, as well as a scissors or knife to cut the cord. Participants are invited to bring a symbol of a "beginning" or "transition" time in their life.

INTRODUCTION

Reader: Rituals are an important way to mark beginnings and endings. Rituals help those in transition to leave behind some aspects of their previous life-experiences or situations and move on to new beginnings. They make it easier to leave behind an old or previous value from childhood, a former family tradition, or a destructive relationship. They help people focus on the newness of acquiring a different job, moving to a new house, beginning a new relationship, or choosing a new value in life.

RITUAL

Invite all to sit in a circle. The leader begins by wrapping the cord around another person. Each one puts the cord around one hand of the next person. The last person ties the two ends together to represent the umbilical cord that unites us all as one. The cord will gradually take on the energy of the group as the service continues. Invite participants to take their symbol of transition, place it in the circle before them, and tell their story. As each person speaks about beginnings and transitions, all help create this collective ritual. This sharing can be done in an informal way, remembering that there are no rigid rules and no one best way to do it. All are equal in creating this ritual.

At the end of the storytelling, each person cuts the cord, takes the piece, and ties three or four knots in it. As each knot is tied, all affirm their transition times in life.

If there is a person in the group who is going through some particular change, ask him or her to sit in the center of the circle. All place their hands on the person, allowing energy and God's power within each person to flow to the individual in the middle. Each person gives a greeting or blessing like, "I give you peace . . . power to rely on your inner capabilities . . . to help you in your transitions."

Bring the ritual to a conclusion by embracing each person in the group, thanking all for sharing the transitions in their lives, and wishing them a blessing as they leave.

By the Sea

PREPARATION

Ideally this service is held near a body of water. A dish of water from the ocean or a lake is needed. Invite participants to bring a reading, song, poem, or drawing related to cleansing or rebirth that they would like to share. Gather people in a small circle.

RITUAL

Lifting the bowl of water, invite each person to think of the negative energy or spirits that they would like to be free from or leave behind them. Remind the group that water is a cleansing element. Pass the bowl of water around the circle and invite the group to imagine they are pouring unwanted negative energy or spirits into the water, saying for example, "I put in this bowl distrust...fear...anger about..."

After the negative energy has been poured into the water, read the reflection below.

READING

Select a favorite passage from Gift from the Sea, *by Anne Morrow Lindbergh.*

RITUAL

The leader passes the bowl of water around and asks all to bless themselves with the water that gives strength and courage.

In conclusion the leader invites one or two people to take the dish of water and return the water to its original body of water. While the representatives take the water, the leader invites all to sing or to talk about the experience.

When all have returned to the circle, join hands in silence. Invite all to feel the warmth, support, and love of God. Visualize ways each will use these gifts.

Love of Land and Country

Have four or more pots of earth in different locations among the people. During the prayer, individuals will bring the earth to a central place where it can be seen by all.

CALL TO PRAYER

Leader: God of our past and our future,
            it is our privilege to join with all creation
            in praising you,
            our wondrous God.

All: You made us in your own image
            and set us in the midst of your creation.
            In ages past, you chose a people
            and gave them a future full of promise.
            When you freed them from oppression
            they brought with them the hope
            that all people are blessed
            and all people could be free.

Leader: This has come to pass in every generation
            for all who have believed that Jesus,
            by his death and resurrection,
            gave them a new freedom in the Spirit.

It happened to our ancestors,
who came to this land
as if out of the desert,
into a place of promise and hope.

All: It continues to happen to us in these days,
as you call us to share
in your peace and your justice.
And so, with hearts full of love and gratitude,
we join with Mary,
a woman of great faith,
in whom we see the fullness of grace.
We join with all our ancestors in faith,
with *N.*, *N.*,
and with all our family and friends
who have undertaken unexpected journeys
in response to your word.
The grace we have known
in the lives of all these saints
is a promise of our own liberation.
We join with them now
as we offer you our praise.

— Adapted from the Preface for
Thanksgiving Day Roman Liturgy

SONG

"Magnificat," by John Michael Talbot, or another song of praise.

READING

From "This Land Is Home to Me" (adapted from the Pastoral Letter on Powerlessness in Appalachia by the Catholic Bishops of the Region).

At two points during the reading, a verse of "America the Beautiful" is sung. At the conclusion of the reading, the final two verses are sung.

(The reading from "This Land Is Home to Me" is found immediately following this prayer service.)

SONG

AMERICA THE BEAUTIFUL

O beautiful for spacious skies,
For amber waves of grain,
For purple mountain majesties
Above the fruited plain!
America! America!
May God shed grace on thee.
And make of us one family,
From sea to shining sea.

Reading continues.

O beautiful for pilgrim feet,
Whose stern, impassioned stress
A thoroughfare for freedom beat
Across the wilderness!
America! America!
God mend thine ev'ry flaw,
Confirm thy soul in self-control,
Thy liberty in law.

Reading continues.

O beautiful for heroes proved
In liberating strife,
Who more than self their country loved,
And mercy more than life!
America! America!
Your people look to you
For justice, peace and dignity,
For freedom giv'n anew.

O beautiful for patriot dream
That sees beyond the years
Thine alabaster cities gleam,
Undimm'd by human tears!

America! America!
May God shed grace on thee
And make of us one family,
From sea to shining sea.

— Text: Katharine Lee Bates (1859–1929);
tune: *Materna,* Samuel A. Ward (1848–1903)

(Some of the above lyrics have been changed to more inclusive language.)

PRESENTATION OF EARTH

Individuals bring forward earth, land that is symbolic of their heritage, their life, and their hope for the future.

In bringing forward the earth, individuals identify its source and offer a prayer, for example:

We bring forward this earth, taken from _____. May it represent all the places in which we have lived and worked. We pray for healing of any pain we have experienced in the past and give thanks for the wisdom, courage, and grace that lives within us now.

We present earth from the garden _____. May it speak to us of the fragile beauty of our planet and our need to tend it with great care. May our efforts serve to bring seeds of life to flourish throughout the earth.

After each presentation of earth:

All: We have loved the people of this land.
            This land and her people are home to me.

SONG

"I Found the Treasure," by Dan Schutte, SJ, or other appropriate song.

READING: *Deuteronomy 30:15–20*

REFLECTION: *Offered by a member of the group*

PRAYER

All: Yahweh, our God,
          you have created us, called us from slavery,
          sustained us through history,
          and brought us to this day and this hour.

          What response can we make to you?
          What response can we make to the sisters and brothers
          you have given us,
          who share our land and your promise?

          Our inheritance is theirs.
          You have given it to us as stewards,
          to share its resources and safeguard its people.

          We admit we have not always done this.
          Today we ask your mercy.
          Restore our sense of kinship with the earth
          and our sense of family with each other.
          Make our land a place of promise and of peace
          for all who seek a home.

          May the future remember these days
          as a time when earth's people
          came to know themselves as a family.

          May we remember these days
          as the time of our recommitment to the struggle for justice
          and may we mark this day as a day of peace.

          We ask this in the name of Jesus,
          who walked this earth and loved its people.
          Amen.

SONG

Appropriate song of praise, joy, or commitment.

READING

THIS LAND IS HOME TO ME
(adapted from the Pastoral Letter on Powerlessness in Appalachia by the Catholic Bishops of the Region)

Voice 1: We write of the people
who live in this land,
people who love nature's freedom
and beauty,
who are alive with song
and poetry.

But many of these people are also poor
and suffer oppression.
The poor of our land
have been wounded,
but they are not crushed.
The Spirit still lives.

Their struggle and their poetry
together keep alive
— a dream
— a tradition
— a longing
— a promise
which is not just their dream,
but the voiceless vision
buried beneath life's bitterness
wherever it is found.

Voice 2: They sing of a life
free and simple,
with time for one another
and for people's needs,
based on the dignity of the human person,
at one with nature's beauty,
crowned by poetry.
If that dream dies,
all our struggles die with it.

This struggle of resistance
is a struggle against violence —
against institutional violence
which sometimes subtly,
sometimes brutally,
attacks human dignity and life.
At stake is the spirit
of all our humanity.

"America the Beautiful" (one verse)

Voice 1:   Once we all
— knew how to dance and sing
— sat in mystery before the poet's spell
— felt our hearts rise to nature's cathedral.

Now an alien culture
battles to shape us
into plastic forms empty of Spirit,
into beasts of burden
without mystery.

And so the church continues,
despite its sins,
working for the poor,
insisting on practical love,
and not just prayers
and good intentions.

Voice 2:   Thus,
there must be no doubt,
that we,
who must speak the message of Jesus,
can only become
advocates of the poor.
This is not to be simplistic,
to see all in black and white,
to be ignorant of economics
and the contributions
of other human sciences,

but in a profound sense
the choices are simple
and stark:

Voice 1:   death

Voice 2:   or life;

Voice 1:   injustice

Voice 2:   or justice;

Voice 1:   idolatry

Voice 2:   or the Living God.

Voice 1:   We must choose life.

Voice 2:   We must choose justice.

Voice 1:   We must choose the Living God.

Voice 2:   More and more people recognize
that a new social order is being born.
Indeed,
the Spirit of God
presses us to this recognition.
We do not understand it all,
but we know we are part of it
   — in this community,
   — in our nation,
   — across the world.

"America the Beautiful" (one verse)

Voice 1:   As this letter closes,
dear sisters and brothers,
we wish you
and all people
the gift of peace.

We urge all of you
not to stop living,

to be a part of the rebirth of utopias,
to recover and defend the struggling dream
of this country and its people.
For it is the weak things of this world,
which seem like folly,
that the Spirit takes up
and makes its own.

The dream of the land's struggle,
the dream of simplicity
and of justice,
like so many other repressed visions,
is, we believe,
the voice of God among us.

Voice 2:   In taking them up,
hopefully the church
might once again
be known as
     — a center of the Spirit,
     — a place where poetry dares to speak,
     — where the song reigns unchallenged,
     — where art flourishes,
     — where nature is welcome,
     — where little people and little needs come first,
     — where justice speaks loudly,
     — where in a wilderness of destruction
the great voice of God
still cries out for life.

"America the Beautiful" (two verses)

Part VI

Resources

Cambridge Women's Peace Collective. *My Country Is the Whole World.* Boston: Pandora Press, 1985.

Cardenal, Ernesto. *Psalms.* New York: Crossroad Publishing Company, 1981.

Chavis, Benjamin E. *Psalms from Prison.* New York: Pilgrim Press, 1983.

Clark, Linda, Marion Ronan, Eleanor Walker. *Image-Breaking, Image-Building.* New York: Pilgrim Press, 1981.

Duck, Ruth C., ed. *Bread for the Journey.* New York: Pilgrim Press, 1981.

Duck, Ruth C., ed. *Flames of the Spirit.* New York: Pilgrim Press, 1985.

Eighth Day Center for Justice. *Cleaning Up Sexist Language.* Chicago, 1980.

Gallagher, Maureen, Clare Wagner, David Woeste. *Praying with Scripture.* New York: Paulist Press, 1983.

Gjerding, Iben, and Katherine Kinnamon, eds. *Women's Prayer Services.* Mystic, Conn.: Twenty-Third Publications, 1987.

Greenberg, Sidney, comp., trans. *Likrat Shabbat.* Bridgeport, Conn.: The Prayer Book Press of Media Judaica, Inc., 1977.

Inglehart, Hallie. *Woman Spirit.* New York: Harper and Row, 1983.

Kirk, Martha Ann, CCVI. *Dancing with Creation.* Saratoga, Calif.: Resource Publications, 1983.

Kirk, Martha Ann, CCVI. *God of Our Mothers: Seven Biblical Women Tell Their Stories.* Cincinnati: St. Anthony Messenger Press, 1985.

Lathrop, Chuck. *A Gentle Presence.* Washington, D.C.: Appalachian Documentation, 1977. (Chuck Lathrop, 705 Virginia Heights, Old Blessington Road, Tallaght, Dublin 24, Ireland).

Loder, Ted. *Guerrillas of Grace.* San Diego: LuraMedia, 1984.

National Council of the Churches of Christ in the U.S.A. *An Inclusive-Language Lectionary.* Readings for Year A, B, C, 1984, 1985.

Neu, Diann L. *Women Church Celebrations.* Silver Spring, Md.: WATER (Women's Alliance for Theology, Ethics and Ritual), 1985.

Oosterhuis, Huub. *Your Word Is Near.* New York: Newman Press, 1968.

Religious Task Force on Central America, *Central America Reflections*. Washington, D.C.

Starhawk. *The Spiral Dance*. New York: Harper and Row, 1979.

Wiederkehr, Macrina, OSB. *Seasons of Your Heart*. Silver Burdett Company, 1979.

Winter, Miriam Therese. *WomanPrayer WomanSong*. Oak Park, Ill.: Meyer-Stone Books, 1987.

Music Resources

The music of the artists mentioned in *More Than Words* is available as follows:

Tom Conry, from North American Liturgy Resources, 10802 North 23rd Avenue, Phoenix, AZ 85029.

The Dameans, from North American Liturgy Resources, 10802 North 23rd Avenue, Phoenix, AZ 85029.

John Foley, SJ, from North American Liturgy Resources, 10802 North 23rd Avenue, Phoenix, AZ 85029.

Colleen Fulmer, from Loretto Spirituality Network, 529 Pomona Avenue, Albany, CA 94706.

David Haas, from Cooperative Ministries, Washington, D.C.

Marty Haugen, from G.I.A. Publications, Inc., 7404 S. Mason Avenue, Chicago, IL 60638.

Daniel Kobialka, from LiSem Enterprises, 1775 Old Country Road, #9, Belmont, CA 94002.

Carey Landry, from North American Liturgy Resources, 10802 North 23rd Avenue, Phoenix, AZ 85029.

Holly Near, from Redwood Records, 4765 West MacArthur Blvd., Oakland, CA 94609, and the Resource Center for Women and Ministry in the South, Inc., P.O. Box 1365, Greensboro, N.C. 27402.

Gregory Norbet, from the Benedictine Foundation of the State of Vermont, Inc., Weston Priory, Weston, VT 05161.

Dan Schutte, SJ, from North American Liturgy Resources, 10802 North 23rd Avenue, Phoenix, AZ 85029.

Marsie Silvestro, from Moonsong Publications, Somerville, MA 02143

Sweet Honey in the Rock, from Redwood Records, 4765 West MacArthur Blvd., Oakland, CA 94609; Flying Fish Records, 1304 West Schubert, Chicago, IL 60614; and the Resource Center for Women and Ministry in the South, Inc., P.O. Box 1365, Greensboro, N.C. 27402.

John Michael Talbot, from Sparrow Records, Canoga Park, CA 91304.

Cris Williamson, from the Resource Center for Women and Ministry in the South, Inc., P.O. Box 1365, Greensboro, N.C. 27402.

Joe Wise, from G.I.A. Publications, Inc., 7404 S. Mason Avenue, Chicago, IL 60638.

Also from Meyer • Stone Books...

WOMANPRAYER, WOMANSONG
Resources for Ritual

Miriam Therese Winter

Illustrated by Meinrad Craighead

"...a groundbreaking contribution. This exciting book addresses the urgent need for ritual which incorporates women's experience. Feminine biblical images of God are recovered; feminine pronouns for God are supplied; valiant women are remembered; the church year is reinterpreted to highlight women's experience; and oppression and violence against women in scripture and society are exposed. I have found a rich resource here!" — Ruth Duck, Editor, *Everflowing Streams*

"For the first time the church prays and sings the ancient story of creation and redemption through women's creative imagination."
— Rosemary Ruether

Miriam Therese Winter is Professor of Liturgy, Worship, and Spirituality at Hartford Seminary, Hartford, Connecticut. She is the author of *Why Sing? Toward a Theology of Catholic Church Music.*

Feminist Studies/Liturgy   264 pp.

Paperback: $14.95 (ISBN 0-949989-00-X)

AGAINST MACHISMO

Rubem Alves, Leonardo Boff, Gustavo Gutiérrez, José Míguez Bonino, Juan Luis Segundo ... and Others Talk About the Struggle of Women

Interviews by Elsa Tamez

The seeds of liberation theology grew out of the oppression of the poor. Now, leading liberation theologians, some for the first time, speak out on the oppression of women.

With unusual vision, Elsa Tamez poses prodding questions that evoke both the issues and the experience of these individuals. Her exploration of the reality of women's struggle, the relationship between women and the church, the contribution of women to theology, and the dramatic influence of feminist hermeneutics results in diverse and searching conversation that breaks new ground.

There is a richness to these interviews that stems from the interview genre itself. These are not formal statements buttressed by footnotes, but rather the personal, spontaneous, insightful, wrestled reflections, feelings, and experiences of Latin America's leading liberation theologians.

Elsa Tamez is Professor of Biblical Studies at the Seminario Bíblico Latinoamericano in Costa Rica.

Theology/Feminist Studies   160 pp.

Hardcover: $24.95 (ISBN 0-940989-13-1)
Paperback: $9.95 (ISBN 0-949989-12-3)

————————

Order from your bookstore
or from
Meyer • Stone Books
1821 West Third Street Bloomington, IN 47401
Tel.: 812-333-0313